Attitude

The Choice Is Yours

By Michele Matt, CSP

Attitude
The Choice Is Yours

By Michele Matt, CSP

Cover Design: Stephanie Stranko www.TaskByTask.net

Graphic Design: Sue Krawchuk Sue.krawchuk@shaw.ca

First Edition ©1996 previously published by Provant Media, Urbandale IA ISBN 1-884926-52-5

Second Edition ©2007 previously published by Book Marketing Solutions, LLC, Traverse City MI ISBN 0-9790834-8-6

Third Edition ©2016 published by Inspiring Solutions, West Des Moines, IA ISBN 978-0-692-02964-0

Library of Congress Catalog Number in Publication Data

ISBN 978-0-692-02964-0

Printed in the United States of America

To purchase additional copies contact:
Inspiring Solutions at info@inspiringsolutions.com or visit www.InspiringSolutions.com

A Word from the Author

Attitudes are everywhere and everything in life! You simply can't go through a single day without them. Your attitude today creates your actions, which produce your results. By gaining control of your attitude, you will gain control of your life. Therefore, the key to getting the results you want in life is gaining control of your thoughts and feelings.

I learned a lot about my attitude from simply writing this book. It took hours of dedication and persistence. It took patience, hope, and a positive attitude to complete the project. I appreciate the confidence vested in me by Todd McDonald and Esther Vanier to write this book. In addition, I appreciate all the support and encouragement given to me by my family and friends. I recognize how important relationships at work, at home, and with friends are to me.

My hope is that this book has touched your life and that you have been inspired to do something differently as a result of experiencing this book. I would love to hear how this book has helped you gain control of your attitude and your life.

Channel the power within!

Michele Matt

Michele Matt, CSP
Inspiring Solutions

Michele@InspiringSolutions.com
Toll Free: 866-225-1249
www.InspiringSolutions.com

About the Author

Michele Matt is known as "The Attitude Adjuster"℠ because since 1984, she has positively influenced the attitudes and actions of thousands of organizations throughout the world . . . inspiring people with practical solutions for positive change at work, home, or play. She founded ***Inspiring Solutions*** in 1991 and each year, she consults with over 150 different groups ranging from training seminars in companies, speaking at conferences, facilitating strategic planning and team building retreats.

Regardless of the type of audience she is working with, Michele has the ability to connect with each participant. She has worked with clients from a variety of industries such as health care, financial services, insurance, technology, government, manufacturing, education and even prisons.

In addition to this best-selling book, she has published several learning resources such as:

- **Activities to Enhance the Good, Bad, and Ugly Attitudes (collection of exercises)**
- **Attitude: A Little Thing That Makes a Big Difference (video)**
- **Attitude Game (training tool)**
- **Bad Apples: Dealing with Difficult Attitudes (video)**
- **Serving Your Customers a Can-Do Attitude (video)**
- **Strategic Planning Handbook**

To order these or other training resources, visit:
www.InspiringSolutions.com

She is an award-winning Authorized Partner for Everything DiSC® and accredited to facilitate The Five Behaviors of a Cohesive Team™ - a learning experience that helps professionals and their organizations discover what it takes to build a truly cohesive and effective team.

A born-leader, Michele has provided state and national leadership in several associations such as the Association for Talent Development (ATD) and the National Speakers Association (NSA). She has been honored as an Iowa Up and Comer and Outstanding Young Iowan.

In 2002, Michele earned the prestigious Certified Speaking Professional (CSP) designation awarded by the National Speakers Association to recognize her commitment to the speaking profession through proven speaking experience, ongoing education, and ethical behavior. Fewer than 300 women in the world have received this designation.

For more information about how Michele can help inspire your people with practical solutions for positive change, call 866-225-1249 or visit **www.InspiringSolutions.com.**

Acknowledgements

The author wishes to thank her family, friends, Dana Annear, Stephanie Stranko, Sue Krawchuk, and the team members at James & Brookfield Publishers for the valuable time, talent, and attitudes they contributed to this book.

How to Use This Book

The primary goal of this book is to help you gain control of your attitude in order to become the person you really want to be. Life is full of ups and downs and peaks and valleys. This book will help you understand how influential your attitude is in gaining control over your life. You'll find that it contains practical yet powerful techniques to help you appreciate, analyze, adjust, and maintain a positive attitude. This book is for you if you:

- Want to gain more control of your life at home or at work.
- Have difficulty accepting change.
- Want to improve your relationships with other people—such as customers, coworkers, and family members.
- Avoid taking risks or accepting challenges.
- Want to enjoy a more fulfilling and happier life.

Like a Good Friend . . .

This book will treat you like a good friend. It will give you advice and ask you questions, but it will not pass judgment on your responses or reactions. In return, try to appreciate and treat this book like a good friend. Open your mind to learn more about yourself and your attitude. You'll grow from the experience. Don't be afraid to admit your areas of difficulty and your frustrations. Be honest with yourself about your attitude.

Use This Book Often

Find a convenient spot to keep this book close at hand as a ready resource. Use the Table of Contents as a quick reference guide. Think of this book as a coach to support your goals, encourage your successes, and re-channel your attitudes.

To fully experience the potential of this book, use a highlighter to mark statements, quotations, or ideas that you find valuable. Answer the questions in the interactive exercises, and jot down notes in the outer margins as you read the chapters. Use the book as a tool to capture your important thoughts and ideas about your attitudes.

The author and the publisher hope that this book truly helps you gain control of your attitude and your life.

Chapter One

How to Understand Your Attitude

Chapter Two

How to Analyze Your Attitude

Chapter Three

How to Adjust Your Attitude

Chapter Four

How to Maintain a Positive Attitude

Chapter Five

How to Deal with the Difficult Attitudes of Others

Chapter Six

How to Gain Control of Your Attitude and Your Life

How to Understand Your Attitude

Chapter Objectives:

- Understand why attitudes are so important in life.
- Explain where attitudes come from and how they are formed.
- Define the components of an attitude.
- Describe and recognize three types of attitudes: Positive, Negative, and Neutral.
- Utilize a formula to calculate your attitude and anticipated results.

Your Lifetime Companions

They've been with you since you were born, and they promise to be with you wherever you go – at work, at home, at school, and even on the streets. Some days, you're glad to have them around, but on other days, you may wish they had stayed in bed! We all have them. Some are good, and some are not so good. In fact, you've been around them so much, you can probably even detect them in other people. We're talking about your lifetime companions – your attitudes.

> Your attitude is your lifetime companion.

Attitude Leads to Success

A recent study by Telemetrics International surveyed 16,000 people. This study linked common characteristics and actions to successful people. One of the most significant differences between high and low achievers was their attitude.

Those defined as high achievers tended to:

- Care about people, as well as the bottom line.
- Respect the value of other people's abilities.
- Seek advice from others.
- Be good listeners.
- Have a positive attitude about life in general.

You Control Your Attitude

There are so many things in life you have little or no control over, such as the weather, the job market, and the economy. But there's one aspect of your life that you do have the power to control, and that's your attitude. Each and every moment of every day, you decide what your attitude will be—about yourself, your job, your customers, your family and friends, change, responsibility, and so on.

> To gain control of your life, you must learn to gain control of your attitude.

Certainly there are other factors that influence your attitude, such as your past experiences and the experiences of those around you. But no one can make you feel anything without your permission. You hold the remote control to the channels of energy that create both your attitude and your results in life.

So, to gain control of your life, you must learn to gain control over your attitude. Having a positive attitude can bring about positive results at home and at work—results that will bring you happiness and success.

What Is an Attitude?

An attitude is the energy that fuels your thoughts, feelings, and actions based on the difference between your expectations and your perceptions (our definition of reality) of that situation. To better understand your attitudes, let's break apart the major components that make up an attitude.

- **Expectations**

  In any given situation, you have consciously or unconsciously formulated a set of expectations, or desired results, for yourself, for other people, and for situations. Sometimes referred to as your standards, these expectations determine your level of satisfaction. The higher your expectations, the more challenging it will be to feel satisfied with any given situation.

- **Perceptions**

  Your five senses and past experiences create your perception, or interpretation, of a current situation. Based on what you see, hear, smell, touch, and taste, you develop your definition of what happened. Your perception may or may not be an accurate account of what actually happened; however, perception is what you use to formulate your thoughts and feelings about the situation.

■ Thoughts

Your thoughts define your state of mind. Happy people are most likely thinking happy thoughts. Conversely, sad or angry people are probably having negative thoughts.

Thoughts spark the formation of an attitude. Once the mind is stimulated, you consciously or unconsciously think about the situation. While they're in progress, thoughts sound like, "I think . . ." Thoughts—like feelings and attitudes—may be expressed out loud or silently to yourself.

■ Feelings

Your feelings keep your thoughts alive. It's virtually impossible to have an attitude without thoughts or feelings. Feelings encourage more thoughts and keep the mind active. While they're in progress, feelings sound like, "I feel..."

■ Energy

The amount of energy you exert in a relationship or a situation depends upon how important the issue is to you. The greater the importance, the more energy you'll use to display your attitude through words, tone of voice, facial expressions, body language, and behavior. Like attitudes themselves, this energy can be positive, negative, or neutral in nature.

■ Action

An action is your physical response to a situation. Once again, you have the choice of taking a positive, negative, or neutral approach to each situation. Your action will be a reflection of your attitude. A positive action in progress sounds like, "I can . . . " or "I will . . . " On the other hand, a negative action in progress sounds like, “I can’t . . . ” or “I won’t . . . ” A neutral action in progress sounds like, “I don’t want to . . . ” or “I don’t care . . . ”

An action is your physical response to a situation.

Attitude Application

The following situation uses the major components to further define how an attitude is created and demonstrated.

- Mr. and Mrs. Davis are celebrating their 15th wedding anniversary at their favorite restaurant. After taking the first bite of his meal, Mr. Davis is very disappointed. He calls the waiter to their table, pushes his plate of food aside, and states in a firm and deliberate tone, “This food is cold and looks like it’s been sitting out all day. I refuse to touch it!”

Based on past experiences from eating at their favorite restaurant, Mr. Davis had high expectations that the food would look appealing and taste good. However, after tasting this particular meal, his perception of the food was just the opposite. He thought the food tasted cold and looked stale. He felt that the quality of the meal was important to the celebration of the occasion, so he exerted energy by requesting that the waiter come to their table (action), and he communicated his attitude by:

1. Pushing aside his plate of food.

2. Talking in a firm and deliberate tone of voice.

3. Complaining about the food.

Check Your

Attitude

Describe a recent situation at work, at home, at school, or in public that led you or someone else to demonstrate an attitude. Complete the following statements to determine what kind of attitude was communicated.

1. Describe the situation by identifying who was involved and when and where it happened.

   Who: ____________________________________

   When: ___________________________________

   Where: __________________________________

2. Define your expectations of what should have happened.

3. Describe your perception of what you believe happened.

4. Identify your thoughts about the situation by completing the sentence,

   "I think . . .

Check Your Attitude (continued)

5. Identify your feelings about the situation by completing the sentence,

   "I feel . . . ____

   ____

   ____

   ____

6. Describe your actions (both words and behavior).

   ____

   ____

   ____

7. Check the attitude that best describes your overall reaction to the situation.

   ❑ Positive ❑ Negative ❑ Neutral

Where Do Attitudes Come From?

Child-behavior specialists generally agree that we develop our attitudes in our formative years—from birth to age seven. The good news is that we all start out with a good attitude; the bad news is that we later learn how to sour our attitudes.

Consider a baby—full of happiness, curiosity, and acceptance. Babies very seldom reject people based on age, race, sex, color, or ethnic background. They're like sponges—hungry to learn, grow, and experience the many facets of life. Unconsciously, babies recognize that they need other people in order to survive.

So, what happens? We become influenced by our environment. Significant people around us—our parents, guardians, family members, teachers, and friends—pass on their attitudes through their words and actions. Studies show that by the time we are two years old, we observe more than 8,000 hours of life—the good, the bad, and the ugly—plus whatever is on TV.

Since we live in a world of constant change, we must learn to embrace change and recognize that what worked yesterday may not work tomorrow.

The Past Is History

Even though the attitudes we learned at an early age are the most difficult ones to change, they aren't etched in stone. We can unlearn them and relearn new ones. Since we live in a world of constant change, we must learn to embrace change and recognize that what worked yesterday may not work tomorrow. And that goes for our attitudes too! Remember, you can control your attitude and your life!

Three Types of People, Three Types of Attitudes

There are as many types of attitudes as there are people in our world. However, for our purposes, we'll simplify things a bit and focus on three broad categories of people and their attitudes.

- **Players**

  Some people are the players in the game of life. They eagerly await opportunities to learn something new and to grow, both personally and professionally. They take risks and are not afraid to make mistakes. Players usually have a positive attitude about life.

- **Critics**

  Another group of people stays on the sidelines of life. We call them the critics. They perceive themselves as experts in the game of life and pride themselves on finding fault in others. They want their complaints to be heard and understood. They often associate with fellow "critics" because they feel comfortable in numbers. Critics usually have a negative attitude about life.

- **Spectators**

  The third type of people go through life watching it happen around them. They're called the spectators of life. Their life experiences are limited because they "play it safe" and avoid risk. They would much rather observe or support others than risk failure or make a mistake. Spectators usually have a neutral attitude about life.

> Players eagerly await opportunities to learn something new and to grow.

People and their attitudes can be temperamental. Just as no one is completely positive or negative all the time, our attitudes can be situation-specific, lasting only temporarily. For instance, a positive person is capable of demonstrating a negative attitude towards a person or situation. Likewise, a negative person can demonstrate a positive attitude from time to time.

A Typical Situation

You're likely to find all three types of people on every "team," whether it's on the job, at home, or in the community. Let's say you've just been put on a project team at work to plan this year's company picnic. The "spectators" on the team will attend every meeting but won't take an active part in the discussion or volunteer to accept any responsibility. They may even attend the meetings to get out of work.

"Critics" will spend most of their time complaining about last year's picnic and criticizing the parameters of this year's event. In addition, they'll probably be the first to shoot down other people's ideas for improving the picnic. And finally, the "players" will engage themselves in the planning and execution of the project.

Check Your **Attitude**

How would you describe your actions lately at home with your family? At work with coworkers and customers? In your personal life? What kind of person have you been? How might the people around you describe your attitude? Place a check mark under the personality type that best describes your attitude in the following environments.

At Home:	❑ Player	❑ Critic	❑ Spectator
At Work:	❑ Player	❑ Critic	❑ Spectator
In Life:	❑ Player	❑ Critic	❑ Spectator

Are you pleased with the results you've been getting at home, at work, and in your personal life? You may need to make some adjustments to become a better "player" at home, at work, or in life.

They'll follow through to make sure good ideas get implemented and tasks get completed. In other words, the players will "take the ball and run with it!"

The Dynamics of an Attitude

To gain a better understanding of these three types of people, let's take a closer look at how their attitudes are formed and communicated. Let's begin by exploring the thoughts and feelings people experience with each type of attitude.

The *"Players"* with Positive Attitudes

The following list describes some of the thoughts of a "player" with a positive attitude:

- There is something good in every situation.
- A problem is an opportunity to do something different.
- Change is a sign of growth.
- A mistake is a valuable step toward success.
- I have control over my life.

> Players find something good in every situation.

The following list describes some of the feelings of a "player" with a positive attitude:

- Happy
- Confident
- Satisfied
- Optimistic
- Loving

The *"Critics"* with Negative Attitudes

The following list describes some of the thoughts of a "critic" with a negative attitude:

- There is always something wrong.
- Other people cause problems.
- Change is a thorn in my side.
- A mistake is a failure.
- I have little or no control over my life.

The following list describes some of the feelings of a "critic" with a negative attitude:

- Anger
- Doubt
- Frustration
- Pessimism
- Hate

The *"Spectators"* with Neutral Attitudes

The following list describes some of the thoughts of a "spectator" with a neutral attitude:

- The situation or the other person is unimportant.
- Someone else will solve the problem.
- Change is unnecessary.
- The future will come and go with or without me.
- I won't even try to control my life.

The following list describes some of the feelings of a "spectator" with a neutral attitude:

- Unemotional
- Tired

- Content
- Indifferent
- Detached

How Are Attitudes Communicated?

The energy from your thoughts and feelings compels you to communicate your attitude through your words and/or actions. You communicate your attitude in three different ways:

- The words you use (what you say or what you don't say).
- The tone of voice you use (how you say what you say).
- Body language and facial expressions (what you do).

The energy from your thoughts and feelings compels you to communicate your attitude through your words and/or actions.

Research tells us that we communicate our true meanings more with our tone of voice and body language than with the words we use. It's been found that only 8 percent of what we communicate comes from our words, and the remaining 92 percent comes from our tone of voice and body language. Let's explore what attitudes sound and look like.

What Do Attitudes Sound Like?

A positive attitude is verbally communicated with action words in an upbeat, enthusiastic tone of voice. Conversely, a negative attitude is verbally communicated with words of resistance in a whining or abrasive tone of voice. A neutral attitude is often communicated through silence; however, it may be expressed with apathy by using passive language.

Listed below are some of the most common words conveyed by each attitude. Read the list to yourself or aloud using a tone of voice appropriate for that attitude.

Positive Language

- I can.
- I will.
- I expect it.
- I will make time.
- Positively.
- I'm sure.
- I choose to.
- Go.

Negative Language

- I can't.
- I won't.
- No way.
- I don't have time.
- Not.
- I'm afraid.
- You made me.
- Stop.

Neutral Language

- I don't want to.
- I might.
- I doubt it.
- I'll see if I have time.
- Maybe.
- I don't know.
- I didn't.
- Coast.

Notice how many "n't" words are associated with negative and neutral attitudes. Learn to eliminate those words from your vocabulary. Learn to think and speak positively. Talk about what you can do for yourself and others, not about what you can't do.

What Do Attitudes Look Like?

Your facial expressions and body language often communicate your attitude more clearly than your words and tone of voice. For example, a smile communicates happiness and a positive attitude. Conversely, a frown communicates anger or frustration and a negative attitude. Hands, arms, and gestures also communicate your thoughts and feelings. For instance, waving your arms frantically in the air communicates excitement, while shaking a clenched fist communicates hostility.

Take a Moment

You've heard and seen them all before—positive attitudes, negative attitudes, and neutral attitudes. Take a moment to describe what attitudes look and sound like coming from the three types of people we defined earlier. What does each type do? What do they say? How do they say it? Describe their tone of voice, facial expressions, and body language.

"Players" with a positive attitude are more likely to take the following action: *(Example)* Smile, laugh, and act enthusiastic.

____

____

____

"Critics" with a negative attitude are more likely to take the following action: *(Example)* Frown and look disgusted.

____

____

____

____

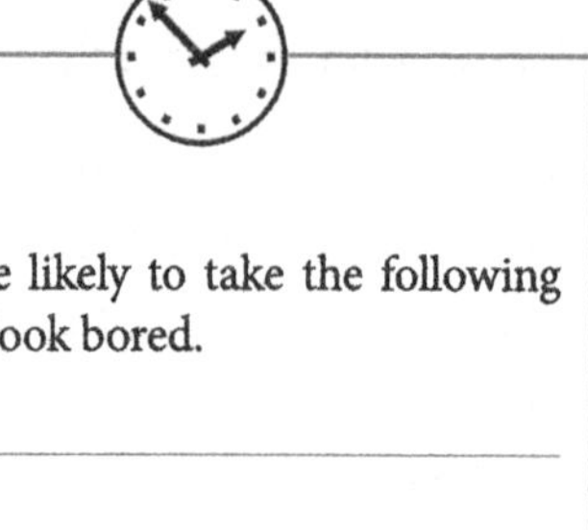

Take a Moment (continued)

"Spectators" with a neutral attitude are more likely to take the following action or inaction: *(Example)* Daydream and look bored.

____

____

____

____

What Can You Expect from Your Attitude?

As previously described, your thoughts and feelings create your attitude. Your attitude determines your actions, which leads to your results. Here are several examples of what the three types of attitudes may lead to in your life.

> A positive attitude can help you achieve a personal or professional goal.

Benefits of a Positive Attitude

Although it's not a guarantee, a positive attitude can help you:

- Get a better job or a promotion.
- Successfully complete a project.
- Achieve a personal or professional goal.
- Satisfy and retain a customer.
- Maintain the relationship of a friend, employee, or spouse.

Consequences of a Negative Attitude

It would be interesting to know how many times a negative attitude caused someone to:

- Be passed over for a promotion.
- Lose his or her job.
- Fail to achieve a personal or professional goal.
- Lose a customer.
- Ruin a relationship.

Consequences of a Neutral Attitude

The apathy expressed by someone with a neutral attitude may cause the person to:

- Miss out on an opportunity.
- Fail to learn new skills or gain needed knowledge.
- Become stagnant in a job or career.
- Fail to develop new relationships.
- Be excluded from an activity.

Attitude Calculation

To gain control of your life, you must first learn to gain control over your thoughts, feelings, and attitudes. To anticipate the kind of action and results you're likely to experience in any given situation, you can use the Attitude Calculation formula described below:

(Thoughts +
Feelings)
x Attitude
____
Action

Begin by assigning a numerical value to your thoughts and your feelings about someone or some situation. Use a 10-point scale, with 1 being extremely poor and 10 being extremely good. Add these values together to arrive at a score for your "perception." With a maximum score of 20, the higher your score, the more favorable your perception of the situation.

The next step is to assign a value to your attitude about the situation, using a scale of -10 to +10. To indicate a negative attitude, select a number between -10 and -1, with -10 being extremely negative. To indicate a neutral or passive attitude about the situation, use zero. To indicate a positive attitude, assign a value between +1 and +10, with +10 being extremely positive.

The final step is to multiply the value of your perception (the sum of your thoughts and feelings) times the value you assigned to your attitude (-10 to +10) to calculate your anticipated action. You'll discover from this calculation that a positive attitude will create positive action. Conversely, a negative attitude will bring about negative action. A neutral attitude, indicated by a value of zero, will result in little or no action.

This Attitude Calculation illustrates how you become what you think. You have the power to choose your thoughts, feelings, and attitudes. By thinking positively, you will enjoy positive results.

Check Your Attitude

In anticipation of the results you may receive from your attitude about something, let's try the calculation formula. Think of a situation you need to deal with in the next few days, and calculate your potential results.

Situation (who and what):

1. Assign a value to your thoughts (1 to 10). ________
2. Add the value you assigned to your feelings (1 to 10). ________

   Your "perception" score is the sum of lines 1 and 2.

3. Multiply by your attitude (choose a number between -10 and +10). ________

Your anticipated actions:

The higher your score, the greater the results and the higher the satisfaction you will likely enjoy. To raise your score, reconsider your thoughts, feelings, and especially your attitude about the situation.

Since you hold the remote control to your thoughts, feelings, and attitudes, you can re-channel your energies by reprogramming the way you think, feel, and act. By changing your attitude toward the other person or the situation, you can improve your behavior or actions in ways that will help you get what you want out of the situation. In the next few chapters, you'll discover techniques for analyzing, adjusting, and maintaining your attitude.

Chapter Summary

In this chapter,you learned how to recognize the three types of attributes: positive, negative, and neutral. You discovered that you choose your attitude through your thoughts and feelings, and that these thoughts and feelings lead to your actions and the results you get in life.

In the next chapter, you'll tune in to your attitudes and discover what you think and feel about the dimensions of your life.

Chapter Two

How to Analyze Your Attitude

Chapter Objectives:

- Use the Self-Image Inventory to assess your attitude.
- Recognize the energy you exert at work, at home, and in your personal life because of your attitude.

Your Attitude About You

The first step in gaining control of your attitude is understanding yourself. Take a look in the mirror. What do you see? Your self-image can be your best friend or your worst enemy, depending on its strength or weakness. Your self-image is how you think and feel about yourself as a person. Your attitude about yourself determines how you act, how you learn, how you work, how you play, and how you relate to others. Your level of self-esteem determines how you cope with problems and fulfill your needs. It measures the degree to which you accept, value, respect, regard, rely on, trust, and confide in yourself. High self-esteem involves having a sense of confidence and reliance in your ability to meet the challenges of life.

> Recognize, appreciate, and, most importantly, believe in your own abilities, and you'll become more confident and capable.

You may compare yourself with other people and become discouraged because you think that others are smarter, better looking, more talented, or richer than you are. This type of comparison isn't healthy and can make you feel discouraged and dissatisfied with yourself. You will always find someone else who is better than you are in one area or another. Think of those other people as role models or inspirations, and eliminate the jealousy you feel toward them. Recognize, appreciate, and, most importantly, believe in your own abilities, and you'll become more confident and capable.

The SI Inventory is designed to help you describe how you think and feel about yourself.

Your Self-Image (SI) Inventory *

The Self-Image (SI) Inventory is a questionnaire that you can use to analyze different aspects of your self-image and self-esteem. It's important to remember, however, that self-image is amorphous and abstract—it lacks specific boundaries or limits and can't be measured on an absolute scale. Think of the following SI Inventory as a subjective indicator of your self-image, not an absolute assessment of it.

The SI Inventory is designed to help you describe how you think and feel about yourself. It is an indication of your self-esteem, your self-perception as it relates to others, and your satisfaction with your role in life.

* Reprinted with permission from *Becoming the Me I Want to Be,* Simmermacher, Don. R & E Publishers, Saratoga, California, 1993.

Directions:

There are no right or wrong answers. The best answer is your honest answer. Avoid answering the questions the way you think others would. Listen to yourself and avoid comparing yourself with other people when you determine your response.

Check the letter of the response that you feel best fits you.

1. In terms of attractiveness, I am:
   - ☐ a. very attractive.
   - ☐ b. fairly attractive.
   - ☐ c. average.
   - ☐ d. fairly unattractive.
   - ☐ e. very unattractive.

2. My personality is:
   - ☐ a. very interesting.
   - ☐ b. fairly interesting.
   - ☐ c. average.
   - ☐ d. fairly boring.
   - ☐ e. very boring.

3. I have:
   - ☐ a. a lot of confidence in myself.
   - ☐ b. enough confidence in myself.
   - ☐ c. average confidence in myself.
   - ☐ d. very little confidence in myself.
   - ☐ e. no confidence in myself.

4. I think that I get along with others:
   - ☐ a. extremely well.
   - ☐ b. well.
   - ☐ c. okay.
   - ☐ d. not very well.
   - ☐ e. not well at all.

5. When competing with others, I feel:
   - ☐ a. I will usually win.
   - ☐ b. I have a good chance to win.
   - ☐ c. I will win sometimes.
   - ☐ d. I will usually not win.
   - ☐ e. I never will win.

6. I dress:
   - ☐ a. very well.
   - ☐ b. fairly well.
   - ☐ c. acceptably.
   - ☐ d. not very well.
   - ☐ e. sloppily.

7. When I walk into a room, I make:
   - ☐ a. a good impression.
   - ☐ b. a fair impression.
   - ☐ c. an average impression.
   - ☐ d. no impression.
   - ☐ e. a bad impression.

8. I accept personal compliments with:
   - ☐ a. no embarrassment.
   - ☐ b. little embarrassment.
   - ☐ c. occasional embarrassment.
   - ☐ d. frequent embarrassment.
   - ☐ e. constant embarrassment.

9. I feel confident that I will succeed in the future:
   - ☐ a. all the time.
   - ☐ b. most of the time.
   - ☐ c. some of the time.
   - ☐ d. hardly ever.
   - ☐ e. never.

10. In terms of maturity, I am:
- ☐ a. very mature.
- ☐ b. fairly mature.
- ☐ c. average.
- ☐ d. below average.
- ☐ e. immature.

11. When among strangers, I feel:
- ☐ a. very comfortable.
- ☐ b. fairly comfortable.
- ☐ c. the same as usual.
- ☐ d. uncomfortable.
- ☐ e. extremely uncomfortable.

12. I feel warm and happy toward myself:
- ☐ a. all the time.
- ☐ b. most of the time.
- ☐ c. some of the time.
- ☐ d. hardly ever.
- ☐ e. never.

13. If I could make myself all over again, I would be:
- ☐ a. exactly as I am.
- ☐ b. about the same.
- ☐ c. slightly changed.
- ☐ d. greatly changed.
- ☐ e. another person.

14. I experience enjoyment and zest for living:
- ☐ a. all the time.
- ☐ b. most of the time.
- ☐ c. some of the time.
- ☐ d. hardly ever.
- ☐ e. never.

15. I admit my mistakes, shortcomings, and defeats:
   - ☐ a. all the time.
   - ☐ b. most of the time.
   - ☐ c. occasionally.
   - ☐ d. hardly ever.
   - ☐ e. never.

16. I feel inferior to others:
   - ☐ a. never.
   - ☐ b. hardly ever.
   - ☐ c. occasionally.
   - ☐ d. most of the time.
   - ☐ e. all the time.

17. I feel that I am in control of my life
   - ☐ a. all the time.
   - ☐ b. most of the time.
   - ☐ c. some of the time.
   - ☐ d. seldom.
   - ☐ e. never.

18. I have an intense need for recognition and approval:
   - ☐ a. none of the time.
   - ☐ b. hardly ever.
   - ☐ c. occasionally.
   - ☐ d. most of the time.
   - ☐ e. all the time.

19. I try to live by my own values, beliefs, and convictions:
   - ☐ a. all the time.
   - ☐ b. most of the time.
   - ☐ c. some of the time.
   - ☐ d. seldom.
   - ☐ e. never.

20. I am able to solve my problems:
- ☐ a. all the time.
- ☐ b. most of the time.
- ☐ c. some of the time.
- ☐ d. seldom.
- ☐ e. never.

21. I avoid new goal endeavors because of fear of mistakes or failures:
- ☐ a. never.
- ☐ b. seldom.
- ☐ c. some of the time.
- ☐ d. most of the time.
- ☐ e. all the time.

22. I believe that I am achieving my potential:
- ☐ a. all the time.
- ☐ b. most of the time.
- ☐ c. some of the time.
- ☐ d. seldom.
- ☐ e. never.

23. I feel that rules or guidelines are:
- ☐ a. to be respected and followed.
- ☐ b. to be used if necessary.
- ☐ c. for others to follow.
- ☐ d. to be challenged or changed.
- ☐ e. to be broken.

24. When someone asks me to do something for them, I feel:

- ☐ a. good, because they trust me to help them; I appreciate the opportunity.
- ☐ b. okay; I'll do it.
- ☐ c. disinterested in helping them; I won't respond immediately.
- ☐ d. bothered by their request; I'll resist accepting the responsibility.
- ☐ e. angry; I won't do it.

Scoring

1. Record the number of responses for each letter.
2. Calculate your score by multiplying the number of each letter by its corresponding value.
3. Add each score to get a total score.

	a	b	c	d	e
1. Number					
x	+2	+1	0	-1	-2
2. Score					

= 3.________
Total Score

Interpretation

Total score of:	Indicates you have:
-48 to -36	A complete feeling of rejection and inadequacy.
-35 to -17	A significant feeling of rejection and inadequacy.
-16 to -1	A negative self-image.
0 to +16	An acceptable self-image.
+17 to +36	A positive self-image.
+37 to +48	A rather inflated self-image. Check your ego.

You've just completed an assessment of your attitude about yourself. It should give you valuable insight into your thoughts and feelings about yourself. The SI Inventory isn't intended to be used as a diagnostic test, but represents an assessment for self-analysis. It can provide a reference point for identifying dimensions of your attitude that may need adjusting.

Your Attitude About Others

Not only is your attitude about yourself important to the results you get in life; your attitude about other people and external factors plays a large part in your overall success as well. You have many dimensions in life—roles and responsibilities to yourself, to your job, to your family, and to your friends. In order to become effective in all of these roles, analyze your thoughts about each situation. Using the scale on the next page, rate your perception of your attitude at home and at work.

Your attitude about other people and external factors plays a large part in your overall success.

At home:

	Negative		Neutral		Positive	
1. About your significant other	NA	-2	-1	0	+1	+2
2. About your children	NA	-2	-1	0	+1	+2
3. About your mother	NA	-2	-1	0	+1	+2
4. About your father	NA	-2	-1	0	+1	+2
5. About your siblings	NA	-2	-1	0	+1	+2

Score: ____________

At work:

	Negative		Neutral		Positive	
1. About your boss	NA	-2	-1	0	+1	+2
2. About your coworkers	NA	-2	-1	0	+1	+2
3. About your company	NA	-2	-1	0	+1	+2
4. About your customers	NA	-2	-1	0	+1	+2
5. About your job	NA	-2	-1	0	+1	+2

Score: ____________

Interpretation

The score for each category—home or work—is the sum of the point values given to its dimensions. A positive score indicates that you're demonstrating positive energies in that aspect of your life. As a result, you are probably enjoying positive results in that area. Congratulations! Keep up the positive attitude!

On the other hand, a negative score indicates that you are demonstrating negative energies and are probably suffering from negative results in that area. A score of zero indicates that you're expending very little, if any, energy in that area. In either case, you'll learn techniques for adjusting your attitude in the next chapter.

Chapter Summary

By completing the analysis of your attitude, you became more aware of your thoughts about yourself and the kind of energy you're exerting at work, at home, and in your personal life. Think of yourself as having a fully charged battery every day. In your battery is stored positive, negative, and neutral energy. Based on your thoughts and feelings about yourself, another person, or a specific situation, you'll exert energy in the form of action toward your life at work and at home.

Now that you have a better understanding of your attitude, what can you do to improve it? In the next chapter, you'll learn techniques for adjusting your attitude.

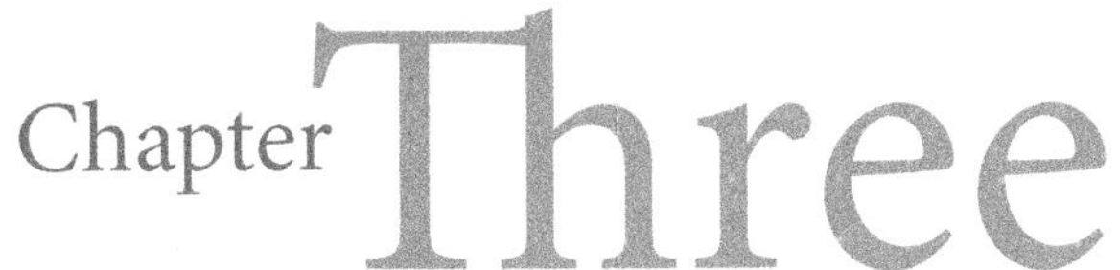

Chapter Three

How to Adjust Your Attitude

Chapter Objectives:

- Utilize five attitude-adjustment techniques to improve the way you feel about yourself, change, other people, and responsibility.

You Are Only an Attitude Away

Do you believe that things simply happen to you . . . or do you believe that you have something to do with what happens to you? If you believe that life happens to you, the most you can do is have lots of luck, insurance, and disaster plans! You'll feel like a victim in the game of life, with little or no control.

However, if you believe that you can influence what happens to you, you'll feel like a "player" in the game of life. You understand that you're accountable for your own attitudes and actions. If you learn to take responsibility for and gain control of your thoughts, feelings, attitudes, and actions, you will gain control of your life.

In this chapter, you'll learn several attitude-adjustment techniques for fine-tuning your thoughts about yourself, dealing with change, and other people.

> If you believe that life happens to you, the most you can do is have lots of luck, insurance, and disaster plans!

These strategies can improve the quality of your life—at home and at work. Regardless of your degree of satisfaction with your life, this chapter holds opportunities for you to adjust your attitude to become a happier, more positive person.

Attitude-Adjustment Technique No. 1:

Listen to Your "Self-Talk"

You are communicating every waking moment of your life. At home, you communicate with your family. At work, you communicate with your customers, coworkers, and supervisors. And when you're by yourself, you're still communicating . . . with yourself.

In fact, even when you're in conversation with someone else, you're communicating with yourself. We call this self-talk. Self-talk is the little voice that formulates your thoughts, opinions, feelings, ideas, and, of course, your attitude! In fact, it is estimated that we spend 50 seconds out of every minute listening to ourselves instead of others!

You probably have heard the computer axiom, "Garbage in, garbage out." Your attitude is formed in much the same way. If you fill your mind with bad thoughts, you'll experience a negative attitude. However, fill your mind with good thoughts, and you'll enjoy a positive attitude along with the good things that come with it.

Self-talk is the little voice that formulates your thoughts, opinions, feelings, ideas, and, of course, your attitude!

We usually live up—or, in some cases, down—to our own expectations. If you think, "I can't," then you won't! For instance, if you expect failure, you may not even try to succeed. On the other hand, if you expect success, you'll work hard to achieve it. Adjust your attitude to strengthen your confidence by eliminating your excuses and self-doubts. Expect success! Channel your self-talk to say, "I can and I will become what I think."

Replace Negative Thoughts with Positive Thoughts

Re-channel your negative thoughts to more positive thoughts. The following chart identifies how to change negative thoughts into more positive thoughts.

Negative Thoughts	Positive Thoughts
I'm a failure.	I've not yet succeeded.
I haven't accomplished anything.	I have learned something.
I made a big mistake.	I was confident enough to try.
I didn't get what I wanted.	I have to do something differently.
I am inferior.	I am not perfect.
I wasted my time.	I invested my time in future success.
I should give up and walk away.	I must work smarter.
I'll never do that again.	I will be more patient.
That was a bad idea.	I will look for a better idea.

Some negative attitudes come from comparing yourself with other people you believe are "better" than you. Your self-talk might sound like, "I can't do that because I don't have as much time . . . I'm not as good looking . . . I don't have as much money . . . I'm too old . . . I'm too young . . . " etc. This kind of attitude comes from thoughts that you're not as good as other people.

You need to think positive thoughts, not negative ones. Picture yourself being a success at what you want to be.

> Picture yourself being a success at what you want to be.

For example, despite Helen Keller's blindness and deafness, she spent her life helping others. Abraham Lincoln failed twice in business, had a nervous breakdown after his sweetheart died, lost six congressional races, and lost the race to become vice president. Yet at age 52, he was elected president of the United States and is now remembered as one of the country's greatest leaders. Why were these people so successful? They were confident, and they pictured themselves as being successful.

Attitude Adjustment

At home, I can or will: ______________________________

____

____

At work, I can or will: ______________________________

____

____

Attitude-Adjustment Technique No. 2: **Pursue Happiness**

If you're feeling sad or depressed about a situation in your life, you may need to adjust your thoughts about it to become happy again. By definition, happiness is a state of satisfaction or contentment. Based largely on your expectations, you determine what makes you happy. Therefore, the higher your expectations, the greater chance for you to experience unhappiness, unless you can find satisfaction or contentment with something less than what you expected. Here are five ways you can find happiness in even the most unpleasant situations.

> Happiness is a state of satisfaction or contentment.

Option 1: Clearly Understand What You Want

The key to your happiness is understanding what's really most important to you—that is, knowing what you want most out of life. Your happiness may often get confused with your desires and things that you believe fulfill your desires. For instance, you might say, "I want a new red convertible." When asked why you want it, you say, "I want to have fun and excitement." The true desire is for fun and excitement; the convertible is simply a means to get fun and excitement.

How many times have you been disappointed or unhappy when something you desired didn't work out or happen the way you'd hoped? For example, if your bank came back to you and said you didn't qualify for a loan to buy the convertible, you might spend days or even weeks feeling sad or depressed about the situation. But if you can quickly recognize that the car was just one means of fulfilling your desire for fun and excitement, you'll be able to think of other ways to bring fun and excitement into your life. Perhaps you'll decide to take a vacation, join a club, or learn a new hobby.

In other words, if you know your true desires, you can create lists of ways to fulfill them. You can have fun without spending a million dollars or find love and happiness without being in a romantic relationship.

> If you know your true desires, you can create lists of ways to fulfill them.

Option 2: Don't Wait for Happiness

Another obstacle to your happiness is waiting until something happens—or stops happening. If you're not content with the current situation, you may tend to believe that a person or a future event will bring you happiness. For instance, you might say, "I'll be much happier when I graduate . . . I move out on my own . . . I lose 50 pounds . . . I get a different job . . . I get married . . . my children move out of the house . . . or I retire."

Stop wishing your life away! You may not have a chance to enjoy tomorrow. Recognize the things at work, at home, and about yourself that are good. Life isn't perfect today, nor will it be tomorrow. Stop waiting for happiness to come to you—it may never find you. Instead, bring yourself happiness today by adjusting your attitude. Think, feel, and be happy!

Option 3: Tell Yourself, "This Too Shall Pass"

Another attitude-adjustment technique for making it through those "blue" days is to remember that pain won't last forever. The suffering or sadness you feel will disappear sooner or later, depending on the severity of the situation. To get through the healing process, tell yourself, "This too shall pass." You've survived other significant stressors in the past, and you will survive others now and in the future.

For instance, do you remember the pressure you faced as a teen—worrying about passing tests in school, completing school projects on time, and getting along with your friends, teachers, and parents? At the time, you probably thought that life couldn't get any worse! To date, you've not only survived those challenges, but probably many others as well.

Option 4: Remember, Others Have It Worse

Self-pity is another form of unhappiness. This kind of self-inflicted sadness often draws little, if any, sympathy from others. One way to overcome feelings of self-pity is to think about how fortunate you are. Think about other people who are less fortunate than you. As long as there is starvation, disease, and violence in our society, there will always be suffering. Think about walking in someone else's shoes, carrying their burdens, and struggling with their concerns. Remember, things could be a lot worse. Stop feeling sorry for yourself just because no one else will!

One way to overcome feelings of self-pity is to think about how fortunate you are.

Option 5: Deal with Depression

The most severe state of unhappiness is called depression. It is an emotional disorder marked by sadness, inactivity, and a difficulty in thinking and concentrating. It's the "down" time in your life. If you suffer from long periods of depression, seek medical assistance.

To adjust a depressed attitude, re-channel your self-talk. What are you telling yourself about the situation? Why are you feeling sorry for yourself? Why are you feeling helpless? Why are you doubting your abilities? What are your opportunities? Who can you ask for help?

The best cure for mild depression is to get up and get doing! Gain control of your emotions. If you can't deal with them by yourself, ask someone for help. Find someone you trust who will listen to your thoughts and feelings. Clarify the role you'd like the person to play. Here are some ways that another person can help:

> The best cure for mild depression is to get up and get doing!

1. Simply listen to you.
2. Listen to you and ask you questions that can help you solve your problems.
3. Listen to you and offer solutions to your problems.

Regardless of the role the other person plays, it's essential that any decision you make is your own. You need to feel that you've regained control of your life. Take one step at a time. Once you re-channel your energy in the right direction, results will follow.

Attitude Adjustment

Think about something in your life, at home, or at work that's making you sad, unhappy, or depressed. Then analyze the situation and try your best to find happiness by adjusting your attitude.

1. What do you feel sad, unhappy, or depressed about?

2. What did you expect from the situation?

3. What are your true desires in this situation?

4. Are you waiting for something to happen to change your feelings? If so, what?

5. Has something like this ever happened before? If so, how do you feel about it now?

6. Can you identify people who are in a worse situation than you are?

7. Who can help you resolve your problem?

8. How can you fulfill your true desires?

Attitude-Adjustment Technique No. 3:
Seek Comfort with Change

Have you noticed lately that, wherever you go and whatever you do, the only thing you can count on for certain is change? It's all around you. There is absolutely no way to avoid change: It affects your family, your career, and your health.

Why is change so difficult to accept? Why do people resist change? The diagram below illustrates your Circle of Comfort and how change impacts it.

Circle of Comfort

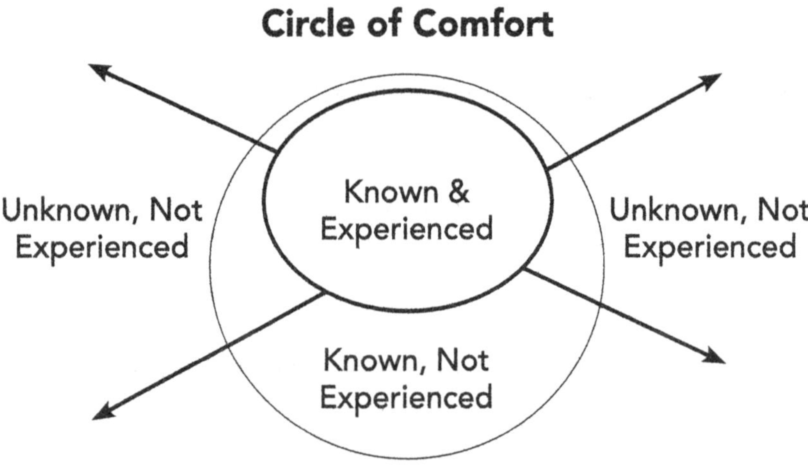

The area inside the innermost circle is called your Circle of Comfort. These are the activities and relationships in life with which you feel most comfortable or familiar. Your comfort comes from your knowledge of—and past experiences with—these activities and relationships. Examples of things you might find in your circle of comfort include activities from your past jobs and current job, neighborhoods you've lived in, and relationships with your family, friends, and coworkers.

The size of your circle of comfort is a reflection of your exposure to the world. A small circle is a sign that you've limited yourself. A larger circle indicates that you've learned and experienced more in life.

The area immediately outside your circle of comfort consists of activities and relationships that you know about but with which you have no experience. You may approach this area with some degree of fear. Examples of activities and relationships in this area include seeking a different job in the same company or joining a professional organization you've heard about from other members.

The size of your circle of comfort is a reflection of your exposure to the world.

The outermost area includes all other activities and relationships—the ones with which you're least comfortable. You have little or no knowledge or experience with these activities and relationships. If you were exposed to one of them, you would feel the most resistance, fear, and apprehension. Some examples of activities and relationships in this area include moving to a new city or starting a new job or career.

If you've recently experienced change and are feeling a bit unsettled by it, here are a couple of ways to find comfort.

Option 1: Face Up to Fear

Begin by recognizing that anytime you face an activity or relationship with which you have limited knowledge or experience, you will be afraid. You learned about fear when you were a child. It sounded like this: "Don't do this . . ." and "Don't do that . . ." Fortunately, this fear probably saved your life on many occasions—when you looked both ways before crossing the street or passed up the opportunity to drink poison.

You used those early frightening experiences to learn what to do and what not to do. It's time once again to use your fear to learn and grow. Think about life as an adventure. Make waves. Don't be afraid to take risks. To risk nothing is to fail to experience life. To risk something is to think, feel, learn, and grow. If you never venture beyond the comfort of your own driveway, you'll miss out on what life has to offer.

Here are four tips for coping with fear:

1. Trust your fear. Think of fear as your friend and companion in life. Let fear guide you, not hold you back.
2. Expect a degree of discomfort at first; it's a natural part of change. It takes approximately 30 days for any new behavior or habit to feel comfortable.
3. Identify the worst thing that could happen if you were to change. Develop strategies for coping with your worst-case scenario so you'll be prepared for the worst if it happens.
4. Get started and take one step at a time. Don't overwhelm yourself by trying to deal with the entire situation all at once. It's important to keep looking ahead and to let yourself become comfortable with each step of the change process.

Option 2: Expect Mistakes

Another aspect of change is dealing with the results you get in the end and along the way. It's often easy to give up on something when it doesn't work out or happen just the way you thought it would. Part of being successful means recognizing that mistakes and failures are bound to happen.

> If you aren't making mistakes, you aren't trying.

Adjusting your attitude to accept mistakes will let you understand them as a natural part of change and growth. If you aren't making mistakes, you aren't trying. It's impossible to succeed without making at least a few mistakes; think of mistakes as the dues of success. Believe it or not, winners make more mistakes than losers. What do you remember most about winners? You remember their victories, not their failures.

For example, Henry Ford forgot to put reverse gear in his first car. Columbus was looking for a quicker route to India when he found America. Thomas Edison made 1,000 unsuccessful prototypes before inventing the light bulb. He said, "I didn't fail 1,000 times. The light bulb was an invention with 1,001 steps."

Mistakes are valuable lessons. They tell you to do something differently.

Mistakes are valuable lessons. They tell you to do something differently. Learn to expect mistakes. Use them as road signs on life's journey to success. The biggest mistake you can make is failing to try—you'll never experience success if you don't try! And remember, if at first you don't succeed, try, try again.

Check Your Attitude

Think of a situation (an activity or a relationship) at home or at work that has recently changed. Analyze why you've been uncomfortable with the situation, and adjust your attitude to accept the change.

1. Identify an activity or relationship with which you're uncomfortable:

____

Check Your Attitude (continued)

2. What do you know about the activity or relationship that might help you feel more comfortable?

   ____

3. What do you fear most?

   ____

4. What do you want from the situation?

   ____

5. Identify the first few steps you'll take to feel more comfortable with the situation

   a: ______________________________

   b: ______________________________

   c: ______________________________

Attitude-Adjustment Technique No. 4: **Value Relationships**

At home and at work, you deal with a variety of people who have a variety of backgrounds, experiences, opinions, and, of course, attitudes. It's virtually impossible to find another person who thinks, feels, and acts the same way you do. Therefore, your attitude toward someone else is largely affected by your willingness to accept and deal with his or her similarities to yourself, as well as the differences.

Teddy Roosevelt said, "The most important single ingredient to the formula of success is knowing how to get along with people."

One of life's greatest rewards, and one of its greatest challenges, comes from the relationships you develop in life. From the moment you're brought into this world until the time you leave, you need other people to survive. And you'll find some of these people more enjoyable than others.

> "The most important single ingredient to the formula of success is knowing how to get along with people."
>
> *Teddy Roosevelt*

What constitutes a relationship? In its simplest form, a relationship occurs when two or more people share something. That something can be a park bench, a sidewalk, a highway, a hobby, an employer, or a house! A relationship may last for several moments or several years. Regardless of its length, your attitude toward the other person affects your behavior and influences the quality of the relationship.

Someone once said, "It's not the length of our life that matters most, it is the depth." In other words, it's not what you do that's important, it's how you do it. How healthy are the relationships you have with your coworkers—your boss, your colleagues, and your customers? How healthy are the relationships you have at home—with your spouse, your children, and your parents? Let's explore several strategies for adjusting your attitudes toward others.

Option 1: Respect Other People

One of the best ways to let other people know that you value and respect them is to ask them for help. Yet, many times your attitude about asking for help prevents you from getting what you want. You may fail to ask for help because of your pride. You may fear that others will view your asking for help as a sign of weakness. If those thoughts have stopped you from seeking others' help, it's time to adjust your attitude!

Just as it makes you feel good when someone asks for your help, others will feel good if you ask for their help. Contrary to what you may be telling yourself, asking questions and requesting assistance:

- Indicates high self-worth and self-esteem.
- Lets others know what you want.
- Gives others the pleasure of helping you.
- Is better for your health, because it releases pressure and tension created by uncertainty.

In fact, by failing to ask for help, you are being stubborn, selfish, and judgmental of others. Not giving someone a chance to help is depriving them of an opportunity to grow.

Check Your Attitude

Identify someone with whom you're having a difficult relationship. List the skills, knowledge, and personality this person brings to your relationship.

Person: ______________________________

Skills: ______________________________

Knowledge: ______________________________

Personality: ______________________________

How can you tell or show that you respect or value this person's contribution to your relationship? (Example: "I appreciate your skills/knowledge/personality.")

Option 2: Forgive and Forget

Another way to adjust your attitude toward a relationship is to forgive and forget past actions. For instance, are you letting something that someone did or said affect your relationship? Forgiveness is one of the greatest gifts you can give someone, and learning to forgive is one of the greatest gifts you can give yourself. Forgiveness replaces negative thoughts with positive ones and prepares you to "give" again to the relationship.

Forgiveness is one of the greatest gifts you can give someone, and learning to forgive is one of the greatest gifts you can give yourself.

Check Your Attitude

Identify someone who did or said something to you that has affected your relationship.

1. On a separate sheet of paper, write down the things that bother you most about the other person.

2. Identify at least five positive characteristics or attributes that he or she brings to your relationship. Don't stop until you have at least five!

   a: __________

   b: __________

   c: __________

   d: __________

   e: __________

Check Your Attitude (continued)

3. In order to forgive and forget:

   a. Throw away the sheet of paper that has the bothersome attributes about the person. Refuse to let those thoughts enter your mind ever again.

   b. Fill your mind with the positive characteristics you identified in Step 2.

   c. Erase the slate and start fresh to build a solid relationship.

Option 3: Communicate Your Expectations

Your attitude toward others is also affected by the degree to which they contribute to the success of your relationship. In the ideal relationship, each person contributes equally. For instance, in a marriage, each spouse assumes 50 percent of the responsibility for the success of the relationship. The challenge with any relationship, regardless of the number of people involved, is making sure everyone feels they are contributing and being treated equally. Inequity in a relationship creates resentment and bitterness.

The key to any successful relationship is open and honest communication.

The key to any successful relationship is open and honest communication. If you communicate your expectations, your chances of having a successful relationship are much greater. Another way to improve your relationships with other people is to follow the Golden Rule—that is, treat others as you'd like to be treated.

Your Golden Rules

Create your top ten rules or guidelines that you'd like others to follow when dealing with you.

When other people communicate with me, I want them to:

1: ________________________________

2: ________________________________

3: ________________________________

4: ________________________________

5: ________________________________

6: ________________________________

7: ________________________________

8: ________________________________

9: ________________________________

10: ________________________________

Now that you've created your Golden Rules, use them when you deal with other people. You'll probably find that what you give to others is what you get in return.

Option 4: Give and Accept Responsibility

As a parent or an employer, one of the greatest compliments you can give to your child(ren) or employee(s) is a sense of responsibility. When you give someone the feeling of being responsible, you're saying:

- I trust you.
- I believe that you can do it.
- I want you to grow and develop.

Having responsibility means that someone trusts you and believes in you. The person wants you to grow and develop from the experience. He or she accepts you and your skills and, most importantly, your attitude. So why are you afraid of responsibility?

To adjust your attitude about accepting responsibility in a relationship, you must first clarify your thoughts and feelings about the responsibility. Do you think the responsibility is important? For instance, if you believe a task is busywork and doesn't serve a purpose, you'll struggle to accept the responsibility. However, if you believe the outcome of the task is important, it's easier to accept the responsibility.

> Take responsibility for your actions.

If you're not aware of the importance of the task, ask. Often, you may be given responsibility by someone who doesn't clarify it or communicate its importance. Take responsibility for your actions. If you don't know why you're supposed to do something, find out!

Service isn't a chore, it's an obligation. President John F. Kennedy said it best: ". . . ask not what your country can do for you; ask what you can do for your country."

Focus on ways you can contribute to or help the relationship, not on what you can get out of it. If everyone on a team, regardless of its size, focuses on adding value to the relationship, everyone ends up the better. Adjust your attitude toward what you can do for others.

Check Your **Attitude** 

Think of a responsibility at home or at work that you've been resisting. Analyze its importance and adjust your attitude toward it.

1. Describe your responsibility:

   ____

2. What is the desired outcome or result of having this responsibility?

   ____

3. To whom is the outcome or result important? Why?

   ____

4. What will you do to deal with this responsibility?

   ____

Attitude-Adjustment Technique No. 5: **Stop "Shoulding" Yourself**

> Guilt is frustration directed at yourself for something you did or did not do.

There is one very damaging and paralyzing kind of self-talk. A voice within keeps telling you, "I should have . . ." or "I shouldn't have . . ." This kind of self-talk is called guilt. Guilt is frustration directed at yourself for something you did or did not do. Your guilt stems from your expectations of yourself. If you fail to live up to your own expectations, you become emotionally connected to the situation by feeling bitter, hurt, argumentative, cranky, testy, or aggravated.

A powerful attitude-adjustment technique is to stop "shoulding" yourself! Re-evaluate your personal expectations. If you believe something is important to you, do it; if it's not important, stop thinking about it and move on. But remember, you can never "should have done" anything. You either did it or you didn't do it. After the fact, you have three choices. You can:

a. Continue to struggle or worry about it.
b. Pretend that you did or didn't do it.
c. Recognize that you did or didn't do it, and move on.

Learn to find peace with yourself. What's over is over. Don't look back—that's not the direction you're headed. Look ahead and plan for the future. Listen to your "shoulds" and do something about them. When you think or say, "I really should do something . . ." your conscience is talking. Your conscience can help you or harm you, depending on how you use it. If you ignore it and do nothing about your thoughts, it will haunt you until you feel guilty.

> Don't look back — that's not the direction you're headed.

Transfer Your Should-Do List

If you listen to your conscience and decide whether it can help you achieve your purpose or reach your goal, it can provide you with valuable information. Next are sample items on a Should-Do List transferred to a To-Do List.

Should-Do List		To-Do List
I really should start exercising.	→	Put a date and time on your calendar.
We should get together for lunch sometime.	→	Schedule the date and time right now.
I should do something to thank them.	→	Send flowers or a card to brighten their day.
I should stop biting my nails.	→	Ask a friend to hold you accountable.

Check Your Attitude

Let's evaluate your Should-Do List. For each item on your list, decide whether it's important enough to do something about or whether you can just scratch it. Then create a To-Do List to help you accomplish the things that are important to you.

Should-Do List	Important?	To-Do List
1.	No Yes	1.
2.	No Yes	2.
3.	No Yes	3.
4.	No Yes	4.

Chapter Summary

In this chapter, you explored five attitude-adjustment techniques for fine-tuning your attitude about yourself, your happiness, dealing with change, accepting other people, and coping with guilt. You learned techniques for replacing negative thoughts with positive thoughts and should-dos with to-dos. You discovered several ways to find happiness and overcome mild depression. You were challenged to face your fears and to expect mistakes during times of change and uncertainty. You gained an appreciation for respect, forgiveness, following the Golden Rule, and accepting responsibility to improve your relationships with others.

In the next chapter, you'll identify ways to maintain a positive attitude.

Chapter Four

How to Maintain a Positive Attitude

Chapter Objective:

- Implement five strategies for maintaining a positive attitude at work and at home.

Preventative Maintenance

Even when you have a positive attitude, you may have experiences at home or at work that drain your positive energy. In this chapter, you'll discover strategies for maintaining a positive attitude in a negative environment and around negative people. Like physical exercise, this is mental exercise that you need to practice on a regular basis.

Attitude-Maintenance Strategy No. 1: **Start Fresh Each Day**

> Start each morning with a fresh outlook on life.

Regardless of what happened the day before or how much sleep you got, start each morning with a fresh outlook on life. As you physically get ready for the day, mentally prepare yourself by deciding what kind of attitude you'll have about the day's activities and the people you'll meet. Remember, you hold the remote control to your thoughts and feelings. The choice is yours, so make it a good one!

Give Yourself a Pep Talk

That's right. Just as coaches give their players a pep talk before a game, give yourself a pep talk before your day begins. Talk out loud or talk to yourself, but use your self-talk to fill your mind with affirmations and positive thoughts and feelings. By hearing your own affirmations, you'll create positive attitudes about yourself and the world around you. Examples of affirmations are:

- I am positive.
- I am enthusiastic
- I am motivated.
- I am happy.
- I am healthy.
- I trust my decisions.
- I follow through.
- I take action.
- I make things happen.
- I can do anything.
- I am lucky.
- I am successful.
- I enjoy life.
- I like myself.
- I am relaxed.
- I accept others.

Always express affirmations in the present tense and begin them with "I" or "I am." Write your affirmations on a piece of paper or on index cards. Put them where you'll see them often, such as on your bathroom mirror, in your daily planner, on your refrigerator, or in your car. Plant your feet firmly on the ground, stand straight with your chin up, look at

By hearing your own affirmations, you'll create positive attitudes about yourself and the world around you.

yourself in the mirror, take a deep breath, and read them aloud, boldly and confidently. You could even record them on tape and listen to them as you travel or do other daily chores.

Check Your Attitude

Think about your affirmations. Brainstorm positive thoughts about yourself, but don't evaluate them. You may or may not believe they're true today, but they're still statements of what you want to believe about yourself. This is the first step toward maintaining control of your attitude and your life.

I am ______________________________

I ______________________________

I am ______________________________

I ______________________________

I am ______________________________

I ______________________________

I am ______________________________

I ______________________________

I am ______________________________

I ______________________________

Come back later and refine your list. Select the affirmations that are most important to you, and write them on a reminder card or piece of paper.

Attitude-Maintenance Strategy No. 2: **Clarify and Prioritize Your Life**

Another way to maintain a positive attitude is to clarify what you want to accomplish in your lifetime. This strategy can help you understand your roles and goals in life. There are four simple yet powerful steps you can take:

Step 1: Clarify your purpose.

Step 2: Visualize your future.

Step 3: Set goals for yourself.

Step 4: Prioritize your actions.

Step 1: Clarify Your Purpose

We've all been given some responsibilities for adding value to life at home, at work, and in the community. Unfortunately, you may not clearly understand your responsibilities to others. You must discover your purpose on your own.

A purpose is a simple, positive statement of why you are here. Like an affirmation, it begins with "I am . . ." but it is a specific description of a role you play in life, such as "I am a happy and healthy person" or "I am a loving and caring husband or wife" or "I am an honest and trustworthy professional."

A purpose isn't a goal statement. A goal is something you can achieve; a purpose is something you fulfill each moment that you're "in balance" with your life.

A purpose is a simple, positive statement of why you are here.

Discover Your Purpose

Give yourself plenty of time and freedom to discover your purpose. Some of the steps you can take are:

1. Identify and prioritize your most important roles in life, such as mother, father, professional, friend, and community leader.
2. List positive qualities that you aspire to, such as being caring, honest, and happy.
3. Narrow your list to a handful of one- or two-word phrases, such as patient and kind, hardworking, and happy and healthy.
4. For each major role in your life, write a purpose statement to describe yourself in that role, using all the appropriate phrases.

Step 2: Visualize Your Future

Once you've clarified your purpose in life, your next step is to create a clear picture in your mind of what you want to accomplish in your lifetime. We all have hopes and dreams. The purpose of this step is to take those dreams and turn them into thoughts that are easy for you to understand so you can become what you think about.

One of the most powerful techniques for achieving your life goals is through visualization. This is the process of creating a mental image of something you imagine happening in the future. The clearer your image, the stronger your

One of the most powerful techniques for achieving your life goals is visualization.

belief and the more likely you'll take action to support that belief. You've heard the saying, "Seeing is believing." Well, if you can see it or visualize it in your mind, you will believe it. Believing in your dreams can motivate you to become what you think about.

An Example

- A high school basketball team needed to improve its free throw percentages. The team was divided into three test groups. The first group practiced shooting free throws for one hour every day for a month. The second group, the control group, did nothing. The third group visualized making free throws in their minds for one hour a day.

  The first group that physically practiced shooting free throws improved their average by 2 percent. The second group, which did nothing, saw their average deteriorate by 2 percent. The group that mentally practiced making free throws improved by 3.5 percent!

This story demonstrates the power visualizing success has on actual results. Whether it's seeing yourself deliver a dynamic presentation to a roomful of people at work, moving into a beautiful home in the mountains, or dropping a 30-foot putt on the golf course, if you can imagine it and believe in it, it can happen!

Check Your Attitude

Think of something you'd like to do, enjoy, or accomplish in your personal or professional life. For instance, maybe you'd like to find the perfect job or career, buy your dream house, marry the perfect person, set an athletic record, or retire in an exotic location.

Close your eyes for a few moments and visualize what it might look like. See yourself doing it and enjoying it. Look at yourself. What are you wearing right now? Where are you? Are others around you? What are they doing?

On a separate sheet of paper, draw a picture of what you visualized. Use symbols and characters to represent your vision so you won't have to use words.

Etch this drawing in your brain. Post it in a spot that will remind you of your vision. Fill your thoughts with your desires. If you can think it and see it, you can make it happen!

Step 3: Set Goals for Yourself

To help your dreams for the future become a reality, set short- and long-term goals. By defining your goals in life, it will be easier to stay headed in the right direction. Goals give you a reason to keep going; you need goals to survive.

> To help your dreams for the future become a reality, set short- and long-term goals.

For instance, in his book *Man's Search for Meaning*, Victor Frankl writes about life in a concentration camp during World War II. He was one of the very few who survived the confinement. In the end, only 1 in 28 people survived. How did he survive while so many others perished? He observed that those who survived weren't necessarily the smartest, healthiest, most fit, or best fed. They were the ones who felt they had something significant left to do with their lives. For Frankl, it was his burning desire to see and touch his wife's face again.

It's critical to have both long-term and short-term goals. Short-term goals help you break up larger, long-term goals into more manageable steps. For instance, a long-term goal may be to retire no later than age 65. Some short-term goals that may help you achieve that goal could be to:

1. Earn a bachelor's degree by age 25.
2. Establish an average salary of at least $30,000 by age 30.
3. Find ways to increase your annual income each year thereafter.
4. Contribute at least 10 percent of your annual income to a retirement account.

A valuable goal statement will meet the following criteria. It will be:

S Specific. It is stated in descriptive terms, not in generalities.

M Measurable. It includes dates and other quantifiable parameters to further define your goals.

A Achievable. It is realistic and possible to achieve.

C Challenging. It presents an opportunity to grow.

For example, a valuable goal statement might be, "I will complete my graduate school program by next May with at least a 3.3 grade-point average."

After achieving a long-sought-after goal, you might feel a letdown until you clarify your next goal. For instance, have you ever gotten a cold after completing a big project? Have you ever stopped doing something completely after achieving a goal, such as reading or running? Your mind, heart, and body become so focused on a task that they become immune to other factors surrounding them. You exert so much positive energy into achieving a goal that, when it's finally reached, you experience an energy surge, or letdown, until you jump-start yourself with another goal.

> To provide steady fuel for your energy, create a list of long-term goals you'd like to accomplish in your lifetime.

To provide steady fuel for your energy, create a list of long-term goals you'd like to accomplish in your lifetime. Break up each long-term goal into several interim short-term goals that will help you chart your progress toward the larger goal. Once you've achieved a goal, celebrate and reward yourself. Cross it off your list and move on to the next goal.

Check Your Attitude

Identify and record some of your long- and short-term goals in life. Write at least one goal for each of the following areas in your life.

Family Goals

By ____________________ I will ____________________

____

In order to ____

Is this goal achievable? ☐ Yes ☐ No

Is this goal challenging? ☐ Yes ☐ No

Check Your Attitude (continued)

Health Goals

By ________________ I will ____________________

____

In order to ______________________________

Is this goal achievable? ☐ Yes ☐ No

Is this goal challenging? ☐ Yes ☐ No

Career Goals

By ________________ I will ____________________

____

In order to ______________________________

Is this goal achievable? ☐ Yes ☐ No

Is this goal challenging? ☐ Yes ☐ No

Step 4: Prioritize Your Actions

The final step in gaining control of your life's plan is to prioritize your goals so you can maintain a positive attitude by simplifying your life. With so many distractions in your life, it can be difficult to keep your priorities in perspective. You have responsibilities at home with

> Prioritize your goals so you can maintain a positive attitude by simplifying your life.

your family; on the job with your boss, coworkers, and customers; and in the community with your church, civic, and professional organizations.

You may feel like the juggler trying to balance several spinning plates on top of a row of sticks. Just as soon as you think you have all the plates (and dimensions of your life) in balance, you start to feel the strain and begin to wobble. Trying to do too much for too many people without taking time to refresh yourself can cause confusion, frustration, and physical and mental fatigue.

Don't complicate your life with things that aren't important to you. Think about how many plates you can juggle in life. Concentrate on the few that are most critical to your happiness and your purpose. Remove the rest. Simply ask yourself, "What can I do today to help me reach my goal?"

Attitude-Maintenance Strategy No. 3: **Enjoy the Moment**

Another way to maintain a positive attitude is to stop worrying about the past or dreading the future and just enjoy the present. Learn to appreciate the things that are going on around you right this moment. One way to enjoy the moment is to think about this saying: "The past is history, the future is a mystery. Today is a gift. That is why we call it the present."

Stop worrying about the past or dreading the future and just enjoy the present.

Here are three options to help you enjoy the moment.

Option 1: Appreciate Life

> Appreciate what you have in life and who you have to enjoy it with.

People who are facing death have the greatest appreciation for the moment. A woman faced with cancer told a class she was eager for Christmas because she was going to make it the best holiday she ever had with her family. Saddened by her situation, the entire class broke down into tears. The woman immediately came back strongly and said, "Weep not for me, but for yourselves. I know this will be my last Christmas, so I will make the most of it. Don't wait until you know it's your last to make it the best. You may not have that chance."

Forget about the past and stop worrying about the future. You've got one chance at making the most of the moment; it will never pass your way again. Appreciate what you have in life and who you have to enjoy it with. Evaluate who and what is most important in your life. To help you with that process, answer the following questions:

Take a Moment

Situation: You were just told that you have one month to live.

1. With whom would you like to spend time during your final month?

   ____

2. If money and health weren't issues, what would you like to do?

   ____

3. If you had a chance to live your life over again, what would you do differently? Why?

   ____

By completing that exercise, you identified the people in your life who are the most important to you. You also identified a goal that was important to your succcss. What havc you bccn doing to achieve it? And finally, you identified an area in your life with which you may not be satisfied. If it's not too late to change, start now.

Option 2: Search for the "Golden Nugget"

Another way to enjoy the moment—especially when you are dealing with a difficult person or situation—is to search for the "Golden Nugget." Regardless of the person or the situation, there is usually something good about everything in life. In some cases, finding it may take time or looking beneath the surface. By recognizing the good, instead of dwelling on the bad, you'll be better able to accept and appreciate the experience.

> Regardless of the person or the situation, there is usually something good about everything in life.

- **Think, "A problem means an opportunity."**

  The first way to find a "Golden Nugget" is to think of problems as opportunities to do something differently. Don't let anything or anyone get you down. Rechannel your thoughts and comments to think more positively about a person or situation. Nothing is ever perfect. To expect perfection is to expect disappointment. Learn to accentuate the positive.

Take a **Moment** 

Let's try it out. For each of the described situations, identify the "Golden Nugget." In other words, think of an opportunity present in each situation.

Situation: You got a bad performance review. Your supervisor identified several areas that need improvement.

Opportunity: ______________________________

Situation: You ran out of gas on the way to work.

Opportunity: ______________________________

Situation: You scorched the dinner you were fixing for your family.

Opportunity: ______________________________

Situation: The electricity in your house went out.

Opportunity: ______________________________

- **Think, "Things could be worse."**

The other way to find the "Golden Nugget" is to look for humor in a bad situation. Perhaps recognize that things could have been worse. For instance, here is an alternate way to think about each of the previous situations:

Look for humor in a bad situation.

1. You could have been fired instead of just getting a bad review.
2. You could have had an 8:00 a.m. meeting that you'd have been late for because of car problems.

3. You could have scorched dinner for your boss and your boss's spouse instead of for your family.
4. You could have been left in complete darkness when the electricity went out if you hadn't had candles and flashlights.

Option 3: Reward Yourself

A final technique you can use to enjoy the moment is to recognize and reward yourself. In any given day, you do so many positive things for yourself and others, such as reaching a goal, exercising, walking the dog, having lunch with a friend, completing a difficult task at work, or fixing dinner at home. You may have forgotten about these things or may not believe that they're of value because nobody said anything to you.

> Don't rely on feedback from others to feel good about yourself.

Don't rely on feedback from others to feel good about yourself. Find inexpensive ways to reward yourself. Perhaps it's taking a nice walk, calling a close friend, or playing with your child(ren) or pet(s). At the end of each day, recall what you did well and rejoice. Feel satisfied with your accomplishments. Remember, even the worst day holds something for you to take away—a lesson to be learned or an idea to do something differently.

To further help you get in touch with your attitude, keep a journal of your thoughts and feelings. This is a great way to express yourself. Chapter 6 includes an Attitude Action Planner to help you get started.

Attitude-Maintenance Strategy No. 4:
Express, Don't Suppress, Your Feelings

Because your attitude is the energy you create with your thoughts and feelings, one way to maintain a positive attitude is to openly express your feelings. Unfortunately, when you were growing up, adults often told you what to do with your feelings. For instance, you were told to "Stop pouting." "Stop crying." "Wipe that grin off your face." "Smile and be happy." "Quit giggling." As a result, you learned to suppress your feelings, whether they were happy or sad, serious or silly.

> Communicating your feelings is just as important as communicating words.

Don't be afraid of what other people may think of you when you laugh or cry. Expressing your feelings is good for your mental health and for your relationships because it communicates your true thoughts about the situation. It isn't healthy for you or your relationships to withhold emotions. Communicating your feelings is just as important as communicating words.

Smile

The most popular way to express a positive attitude is through a warm, sincere smile. When you smile, you communicate your happiness. It's a symbol of contentment and satisfaction.

Did you know that it's virtually impossible to think negative thoughts while you're smiling? Try it out. Think of someone or something that really made you mad. Create a picture in your mind. Now smile. Could you do it?

Take a long, slow, deep breath and smile. Feel good about yourself, the people around you, and your environment. The beauty of a smile is that it not only makes you feel good, but seeing your smile makes others feel good too. A smile is a sign of acceptance and appreciation. It says, "I'm glad to see you, and I respect you as a person." Therefore, if you extend a smile to someone, you're likely to get a smile in return.

Laughter: A Healthy Mental Workout

Another great way to express a positive attitude and relieve pain is to laugh. You can laugh only when you're relaxed, and the more relaxed you are, the less pain you feel. When you laugh, endorphins are released in your brain that give you a "natural high," and your respiratory system gets a workout comparable to exercise.

As you learned earlier, you had a great attitude as a child. You knew a lot more about having a good time than most adults. Adults tend to take life too seriously. If you make time to play, dance, sing, and laugh, you'll always be a kid at heart—and being a kid again is good for your heart. Discover what makes you laugh. Some examples include reading cartoons or comic books, watching funny movies, listening to comedians, or playing with children or pets. A mental workout of laughter is just as important as a physical workout of exercise.

Having a sense of humor can often break up a stressful situation.

Having a sense of humor can often break up a stressful situation. Being able to laugh at yourself or a relationship can help you accept or make the most of even the worst situations.

Cry

Another way to express your feelings is through tears. When was the last time you had a good cry? Tears are a natural part of the healing process, and crying is just as important for releasing your feelings when you're sad as laughing is when you're happy. Give yourself time to heal from an emotional wound.

Attitude-Maintenance Strategy No. 5: **Surround Yourself with Positive Influences**

The final strategy for maintaining a positive attitude is to surround yourself with positive influences. Your thoughts and feelings are most easily influenced through your senses—that is, from what you see, hear, smell, touch, and taste. Here are some tangible ways you can create a positive environment for yourself and others at work and at home by appealing to your senses.

Take a **Moment**

Identify three situations at home or at work where expressing your feelings is difficult. Describe how you can better communicate your feelings to maintain a healthy attitude.

	Situation	Express
1.		
2.		
3.		

Positive Images

- ☐ Decorate your office and home with your favorite photographs of family and friends.
- ☐ Display plaques, certificates, and trophies of your accomplishments.
- ☐ Post your favorite poems, cartoons, and quotes.

Positive Sounds

- ☐ Listen to music that's appropriate to your desired feelings — upbeat music for energy or soothing music to relax.
- ☐ Sit outside and tune in to the sounds of nature—the wind, the rain, the birds, or the waves.
- ☐ Find a quiet spot to meditate or just listen to yourself think.

Positive Smells

- ☐ Burn scented candles.
- ☐ Bake bread or pastries.
- ☐ Arrange or buy a bouquet of fresh flowers.

Positive Feelings

- ☐ Hug or kiss someone.
- ☐ Exercise your body regularly—take a walk, jog, play golf or tennis, lift weights.
- ☐ Take a bubble bath or sit in a hot tub to relax.

Positive Tastes

- ☐ Eat regularly and maintain a balanced diet.
- ☐ Drink plenty of water each day to cleanse your system.
- ☐ Treat yourself to your favorite meal or dessert as a reward for doing something good.

Check Your Attitude

Select several strategies for maintaining a healthy attitude through your senses. Refer to the previous list of ideas and add your own.

Positive Images

1. ______________________________

2. ______________________________

Positive Sounds

1. ______________________________

2. ______________________________

Positive Smells

1. ______________________________

2. ______________________________

Positive Feelings

1. ______________________________

2. ______________________________

Positive Tastes

1. ______________________________

2. ______________________________

Chapter Summary

This chapter presented five strategies to maintain a positive attitude. You learned how to start and end each day with positive thoughts. You explored the importance of setting goals for the future, while enjoying the moment. In addition, you were challenged to express your true feelings about life's ups and downs. With time and practice, these attitude-maintenance strategies will help you gain control of your attitude and your life.

Do you live with or work with someone who has an attitude problem? In the next chapter, you'll learn a process for dealing with the difficult attitudes of others.

Chapter Five

How to Deal with the Difficult Attitudes of Others

Chapter Objectives:

- Understand why difficult attitudes can cause conflict.
- Identify the four choices you have in dealing with someone's difficult attitude.
- Utilize a five-step process for dealing with a difficult attitude.

It's much easier to maintain a positive attitude when you're surrounded by or you deal with people who have a positive attitude. In this chapter, you'll explore strategies for re-channeling the negative energy created by another person's difficult attitude in order to maintain and control your positive attitude.

Difficult Attitudes

> You can encounter difficult people anywhere.

Difficult people—you may encounter them at home, at work, in a store, on the telephone, or even while driving down the highway. You may refer to them as "Sassy Suzy," "Defiant Dave," "Carol Complainer," "Roger Rough," "Nellie Never-Work," "Howard Who-Cares," or "Edward Ego"! Regardless of their attitudes, your goal in dealing with them is to maintain your attitude and not let them get you down.

Your Choices

People like to have choices. You like to choose the clothes you wear, the food you eat, the city you live in, and the job you have. From reading this book, you've learned that you also have your choice of attitudes.

When you deal with someone who has a different or difficult attitude, you have four choices, depending on how important the person and the outcome of his or her behavior are to you.

Option 1: Disregard the Person and Remove Yourself

If the other person isn't important to you, your first choice in dealing with the difficult attitude is to ignore it. For example, you may disregard a complete stranger's difficult attitude in a public setting because you have no vested interest in a relationship with him or her.

Option 2: Accept the Person and Remove Yourself

If your relationship with the other person is important, you may have more of an interest in his or her well-being. To maintain your relationship, you accept the person for who he or she is, but at the present time, you decide not to worry about or take action regarding his or her attitude or behavior. For instance, it may be the first time he or she has acted this way, or you may have other priorities that prevent you from investing time in dealing with the situation.

Option 3: Accept the Person and Understand His or Her Attitude

Your third choice in dealing with someone's difficult attitude is to accept the person and try to understand his or her attitude. Until you take the time to understand how the other person thinks and feels about a situation, you may pass incorrect judgments or make false assumptions about him or her. By investing your time in asking questions and listening with an open mind, you'll gain a greater understanding of the reasons behind the attitude or behavior.

Option 4: Influence the Person's Attitude and Behavior

The final and, perhaps, most challenging way to deal with someone's difficult attitude is to try to influence the attitude and change the behavior. The reason this option is the most difficult is that, just as you have control over your attitude, other people have control over their attitudes too. You can only do or say things that can influence others' thoughts and feelings; others choose their own attitudes and actions.

Changing Attitudes

It is important to know that you may be able to change someone's behavior without affecting a change in the person's attitude. For example, a seven-year-old boy is asked to clean his bedroom. Although he may clean it because his mom told him to, he still may think and feel that it's a frivolous task.

> Changing behavior without changing the underlying attitude is a "bandage approach" to changing a habit.

Changing behavior without changing the underlying attitude is a "bandage approach" to changing a habit. It's a short-term solution. The problem is most likely going to recur. To effect a long-term solution, you must get the person to change his or her attitude as well as behavior.

Steps for Dealing with Someone's Difficult Attitude

The model on the next several pages illustrates and explains a five-step process for dealing with someone else's difficult attitude. The steps are:

Step 1:	Determine your involvement.
Step 2:	Understand the other person.
Step 3:	Influence the other person's attitude.
Step 4:	Resolve the problem.
Step 5:	Recover.

Examples of relationships that can benefit from using this model are those between or among:

- Parent and child
- Teacher and student
- Husband and wife
- Supervisor and employee
- Employee and customer
- Friends
- Relatives
- Peers
- Coworkers

Step 1:
Determine Your Involvement

Once you observe someone's difficult attitude, the first step is to determine what, if any, involvement you want with the situation.

There are several critical questions you can answer to help determine this. It's important to answer these questions on your own, perhaps in private, prior to confronting the person.

Question 1: Is this person important to you?

The first question identifies the importance of your relationship with the other person. Do you care about this person? Are you responsible for his or her behavior and well-being? For example, a parent cares for and is responsible for his or her child(ren). A supervisor is responsible for managing the behavior of his or her employee(s). An employee is concerned about the happiness of his or her customer. In these situations, you would answer the question "Yes" and move on to the next question.

Remove Yourself

If you answer "No" to any of the questions in Step 1, you remove yourself from the situation or the relationship simply by walking away or not responding to the other person's attitude or behavior. This option is crucial to maintaining your positive attitude. It's not a sign of weakness. Actually, it takes more strength to leave and let go than to stay in an unhealthy relationship.

Question 2: Has This Happened Before?

Everyone is entitled to an occasional bad-attitude day. If this is the first time you've ever observed this kind of attitude or behavior from the other person, you may not want to worry about it. If so, answer this question "No" and remove yourself.

Everyone is entitled to an occasional bad-attitude day.

On the other hand, if you've observed this type of attitude before, you may want to deal with it to stop it from happening again. Bad habits are best broken in the early stages of their development. Therefore, ask yourself the next question.

Question 3: Does This Bother You?

For every action, there is usually some type of reaction. Thus, if this behavior bothers you, it's best to deal with it instead of bottling up your thoughts and feelings. To avoid overreacting, you may want to give yourself some time to think about the situation before you answer this question. Often, a problem doesn't seem as severe the next day. However, if you have strong feelings about the situation, move on to the last question. But if you can tolerate the attitude or behavior, remove yourself.

Question 4: Are You Willing to Invest Your Time?

The final question addresses your willingness to take the time to carefully and accurately communicate with the other person. If this isn't a good time or place to acknowledge the attitude, you may want to defer dealing with it for now and come back to it at a more appropriate or convenient time. For instance, it's not good to deal with a difficult attitude if someone is walking out the door. Make sure you'll have enough time to thoroughly deal with the issue.

Prepare to Communicate

If you answered "Yes" to all the questions in Step 1, you determined that this person is important to you; this behavior has happened before; it bothers you; and you are willing to confront the person about it. Before you go on to Step 2, make sure you're ready to communicate.

- Do you have all the facts about the behavior (dates, places, number of occurrences)?
- Are you in control of your emotions?
- Is this an appropriate time and place?

Gather and write down all the facts about the behavior to make sure you properly describe what happened. Also, write down questions you want to ask. Take this documentation with you.

> Gather and write down all the facts about the behavior to make sure you properly describe what happened.

Avoid discussing the situation when you and the other person are upset or angry. Calm down. If that's not possible, find a quiet location where you can discuss the situation in private. Avoid embarrassing the other person by dealing with the problem in front of others, such as peers, coworkers, or customers.

Check Your Attitude

1. Think of someone with a difficult attitude who prompted you to simply get up and remove yourself from the situation.

____

____

2. Why did you decide not to get involved?

____

____

Step 2:
Understand the Other Person

The goal of this step is to help you empathize with the other person. That doesn't mean you have to agree with him or her. You just need to understand the person's situation and accept them without passing judgment or making incorrect assumptions.

Ask Questions and Listen to Empathize

The only way to better understand someone and validate your perceptions is to learn more about the situation. It's important to keep an open mind and a closed mouth during this step. Ask open-ended questions to learn the other person's thoughts and feelings about the situation. Ask who, what, where, when, why, and how questions to better understand what compelled the attitude and behavior.

The only way to better understand someone and validate your perceptions is to learn more about the situation.

Summarize the Person's Thoughts and Feelings

After the other person has shared his or her thoughts and feelings about the situation, confirm your understanding by restating the main points. Communicate that you understand what the person thinks and feels about the situation. You don't have to agree with the thoughts and feelings—just empathize with the situation.

The model for this summary sounds like: "(Person's first name), I understand why you feel (summarize his or her feelings) and that you think (summarize his or her thoughts)."

Accept the Person

In Step 1, you determined that this person was important to you. Therefore, Step 2 seeks to maintain that relationship. When you accept someone, you're not necessarily committing to liking or even respecting the person. You're simply agreeing to accept the person for who they are, regardless of their opinions, personality, attitudes, and behavior.

Do You Desire a Change in Attitude and Behavior?

The final part of Step 2 is to determine whether you'd like a change in the person's attitude and behavior. Notice that this doesn't occur until after you've discussed his or her thoughts and feelings. Through your conversation, you may have clarified misunderstandings or incorrect assumptions. Without completely understanding the other person's viewpoint, you may make inappropriate comments or suggestions.

> Without completely understanding the other person's viewpoint, you may make inappropriate comments or suggestions.

If you feel that a change in the person's attitude and behavior is no longer necessary, terminate the conversation by:

1. Expressing your appreciation for his or her feedback.
2. Offering future assistance or guidance.

On the other hand, if you still believe that a change is desirable, continue to Step 3.

Check Your **Attitude**

1. Think of someone with a difficult attitude with whom you recently spent time in an effort to understand his or her thoughts and feelings.

 ____

 ____

2. What did you learn from your discussion?

 ____

 ____

3. Did your conversation change your perceptions of the person's attitude? If so, how?

 ____

 ____

Step 3:
Influence the Person's Attitude

The purpose of Step 3 is to help the other person recognize that his or her attitude is causing a problem. Without agreement that a problem exists, it will be virtually impossible to effect an attitude change.

Describe How You Feel

First, let the other person know how you feel about the situation. A quality relationship demands open and honest communication from both individuals. Since you spent Step 2 listening to the other person's thoughts and feelings, he or she should be more willing to listen to your feelings.

Begin by acknowledging the behavior that bothers you, then describe how it makes you feel. The format of this discussion might be:

Begin by acknowledging the behavior that bothers you, then describe how it makes you feel.

- "(*Person's first name*), when you (*describe the attitude or behavior you observed*), it makes me feel (*describe your feelings*), because I think (*describe your thoughts about the situation*)."

Explain Possible Consequences

You need to let the other person know what has happened or what might happen in the future if his or her attitude and behavior continue. Let them know what privileges may be lost if the behavior continues. Make sure that you're willing and able to enforce the consequences you impose. This is no time for idle threats.

Suggest Other Ways to Think About It

Help the other person gain a broader perspective on the situation. Offer a more positive way to think about it and his or her contribution. Identify the benefits of handling the situation with more positive behavior. In addition, you may tell the person how his or her difficult behavior affects other people, such as coworkers, customers, siblings, friends, and parents.

Invite a Reaction

Since you're trying to influence the other person's attitude, it's important to have him or her respond to your suggestions. Ask open-ended questions to elicit feelings about your suggestions. Then ask closed-ended questions to confirm his or her understanding that a problem exists. Examples of such questions are:

> Ask open-ended questions to elicit feelings about your suggestions.

Open-ended questions:	Closed-ended questions:
■ "What do you think?"	■ "Would you agree?"
■ "How do you feel about that?"	■ "Do you know how to do it?"
■ "Why is that important to you?"	■ "Can you see my point of view?"

Gain Agreement That There's a Problem

The last part of Step 3 asks you to mutually agree that a problem exists. From your conversation, you might have discovered that the problem is the result of one of several things, such as:

- Lack of adequate training
- Inadequate communication
- Incorrect information
- Misunderstandings
- Unclear roles and responsibilities
- Unreasonable expectations

Be sensitive to the ownership of the problem. Using words and phrases like, "You need to . . . " or "Your problem is . . . " tends to put the other person on the defensive instead of preparing him or her to deal with the problem.

Share responsibility for fixing the problem.

Use sentences that begin with "We . . . " and "Our . . . " instead of "You . . . " to indicate your willingness to support and coach the other person. Share responsibility for fixing the problem. Move on to Step 4 after you receive agreement that a problem exists.

Check Your Attitude

Identify the most common difficult attitudes you encounter. Then describe how those attitudes make you feel.

Types of difficult attitudes (*Example: Complainers and whiners*)

____

____

____

____

That behavior makes me feel (*Example: Frustrated and sidetracked*)

____

____

____

____

Step 4:
Resolve the Problem

The purpose of this step is to determine possible solutions to the attitude or behavior problem by defining expectations for a similar situation in the future.

Define Future Expectations

To define your priorities, as well as the other person's, Step 4 asks you to determine what you're trying to accomplish. Your description, or goal statement, should summarize what's important to you and what's important to the other person. Through negotiation, you must arrive at a specific definition of the desired solution. In some cases, there may be no room for negotiation, such as when you're dealing with company policies and procedures, laws, and other rules.

Through negotiation, you must arrive at a specific definition of the desired solution.

Mutually Discuss Solutions

Ask the other person to offer solutions for meeting the defined expectations in order to correct the problem or prevent it from happening again. The more ideas the other person contributes, the more likely it is he or she will accept responsibility for changing his or her difficult behavior. Offer your own solutions too. Don't evaluate or discredit any ideas until you've explored all possible solutions. Keep an open mind!

Agree on the Best Solution

After you've exhausted and evaluated all possible solutions, decide which one best meets the criteria you established earlier. Whenever possible, ask the other person to select the best solution; that way, you'll get him or her to take ownership of the problem and agree to the change you desire.

> Whenever possible, ask the other person to select the best solution.

If you're a supervisor, you may not have as many options to choose from due to the performance requirements of the job. So be specific about your expectations, and recognize your right and responsibility to disagree with and even veto the other person's recommendations.

Check Your Attitude

Think of a current difficult attitude you're dealing with at home or at work.

1. Describe what you expect from the situation or the other person, and why.

____

____

2. List as many solutions as you can for meeting your expectations. Don't evaluate your ideas, just record them all.

____

____

Step 5:
Recover

The final step in dealing with someone's difficult attitude is to recover from the experience and move on. This step occurs after the face-to-face discussion.

Regain Your Positive Attitude

At this point, you may feel frustrated, angry, disappointed, sad, or betrayed by the other person's difficult attitude. The first part of the recovery step is to bring your attitude back to the level of contentment or happiness you felt before.

Let go of your own negative feelings about the person. Separate the behavior from the person. In Step 1, you admitted that this person was important to you. Don't let this confrontation damage that relationship. Tell yourself, "I like the person. It's his or her behavior that I dislike."

> Let go of your own negative feelings about the person.

Follow Through with Your Commitments

Now you need to follow through with any commitments you made during the problem-solving portion of your conversation. If you agreed to help resolve the problem, do what you said you'd do. While you're at it, don't forget to monitor how the other person is doing on his or her commitments.

Recognize Changes in Attitude and Behavior

Encouragement is a large part of this final step. If you don't see an immediate change in the other person's attitude or behavior, practice patience. It takes time to change a habit. Give praise and encouragement for effort, not just accomplishment.

On the other hand, if you haven't seen a change over a reasonable time, confront the other person about his or her difficult attitude or behavior. Begin again with Step 1 to determine the extent of your involvement. After all, things may have changed. After several confrontations with the other person, where little or no change is made, simply terminate the relationship.

Chapter Summary

In this chapter, you learned a powerful five-step process for dealing with other people who have difficult attitudes or attitudes that are simply different from yours. You discovered that you have a choice in dealing with other people's attitudes to preserve your own positive attitude. It's important that you don't let someone else's bad attitude influence your own good attitude.

Before using the five-step process, remember to consider how your attitude may influence the situation. It's always easy to think that the other person has the attitude problem. Examine your own attitude and make appropriate adjustments before you confront the other person.

In Step 1, ask yourself several questions to determine your involvement. You can remove yourself from the situation if the person is unimportant, if this is the first time you've observed the difficult behavior, or if the situation simply doesn't bother you. Conversely, if you're willing to invest the time to properly deal with the situation, Step 2 explains how to understand the other person by asking questions and listening to empathize with him or her. If you desire a change, the next step is to influence his or her attitude. Once you gain an agreement that there is a problem,

Step 4 shows you how to resolve the problem. Step 5 explains how to recover and regain your positive attitude.

Next, you'll have the opportunity to practice the five-step process.

As you learned earlier, attitudes are everywhere. Think of someone who has an especially difficult attitude. Now use the space below to record your strategy for dealing with his or her bad attitude using the five-step process you just learned.

Step 1: **Determine Your Involvement**

1. Is this person at all important to you? If so, why?

   ____

2. Has this happened before? When and how often?

   ____

3. Does it bother you? If so, why?

   ____

4. Are you willing to invest your time? If so, when will you discuss it?

   ____

Step 2: **Understand the Other Person**

1. Ask questions and listen to empathize. (Write out who, what, when, where, why, and how questions to ask the other person.)

____

____

2. Summarize his or her thoughts and feelings. (You won't be able to do this until you have had your discussion.)

3. Accept the person.

4. Do you desire a change in the person's attitude and behavior? (You won't be able to answer this question until you have had your discussion.)

Step 3: **Influence the Other Person's Attitude**

1. Describe how you feel.

"______________, when you______________________________
Person's name *(describe the attitude or behavior you observed)*

it makes me feel ______________________________,
(describe your feelings)

because I think ______________________________."
(describe your thoughts about the situation)

2. Explain each of the potential consequences.

____

____

3. Suggest other ways to think about the situation.

4. Invite a reaction from the other person. (Record his or her reaction.)

5. Gain agreement that there is a problem. (Record his or her agreement)

Step 4: **Resolve the Problem**

1. Define future expectations. (Record the things that you want, and the other person's expectations during your discussion.)

2. Mutually discuss solutions. (Record some of your thoughts, but be sure to ask for the other person's ideas during the discussion.)

____

____

3. Agree on the best solution. (Record the mutual solution.)

____

____

Step 5: **Recover**

1. Regain your positive attitude. (Identify strategies for adjusting or maintaining your positive attitude.)

____

____

2. Follow through with the commitments you promised.

____

____

3. Recognize any change in the other person's attitude and behavior.

Chapter Six

How to Gain Control of Your Attitude and Your Life

Chapter Objectives:

- Assess your understanding of your attitude.
- Learn how to use the Attitude Action Planner to gain control of your attitude and your life.

This book has exposed you to the essential knowledge and tools for gaining control of your attitude and your life. This chapter will evaluate your confidence in using this knowledge and tools.

Self-Test

After reading this book and completing the interactive exercises, I can . . .

Topic	**Level of Confidence**
Attitude Awareness	Low — High
1. Identify the major components of an attitude.	1 2 3 4 5
2. Describe the three types of attitudes.	1 2 3 4 5

Topic	Level of Confidence
Attitude Awareness	Low — High
3. Explain why attitudes are so important.	1 2 3 4 5

If you don't know how to understand your own attitude, review Chapter 1.

Attitude Analysis	Low — High
4. Evaluate my self-image.	1 2 3 4 5
5. Rate my attitude at home and at work.	1 2 3 4 5

If you don't know how to analyze your own attitude, review Chapter 2.

Attitude Adjustment	Low — High
6. Explain how to gain control of my attitude and my life.	1 2 3 4 5
7. Describe at least five attitude-adjustment techniques.	1 2 3 4 5
8. Identify at least three ways to find happiness.	1 2 3 4 5
9. Explain at least three ways to improve my relationships with other people.	1 2 3 4 5

If you don't know how to adjust your attitude, review Chapter 3.

Topic	Level of Confidence				
Attitude Maintenance	Low				High
10. Describe at least five attitude-maintenance strategies.	1	2	3	4	5
11. List the four steps to prioritizing my life.	1	2	3	4	5
12. Explain three ways to enjoy the moment.	1	2	3	4	5
13. List at least five techniques for surrounding myself with positive influences.	1	2	3	4	5

If you don't know how to surround yourself with positive influences, review Chapter 4.

Attitude of Others	Low				High
14. Recognize the four choices I have in dealing with another person's bad attitude.	1	2	3	4	5
15. Explain the five-step program for dealing with another person's bad attitude or behavior.	1	2	3	4	5

If you don't know how to deal with other people's difficult attitudes, review Chapter 5.

Be Prepared

Before you attempt to gain control of your attitude and your life, you must be aware of several critical factors that will affect your success.

1. You must have the desire to change your attitude and your bad habits. Just think of all the benefits to you and others if you do change!
2. Be patient with yourself. Don't expect immediate results. Anytime you change a habit, your natural tendency is to resort to your old bad habits. Give yourself time to adjust.
3. Change takes a lot of dedication and work to be effective. Take one step at a time. If at first you don't succeed, try, try again.
4. The process of change is continuous; it's never complete. As soon as you stop changing, you stop growing. Make a commitment to lifelong learning.
5. Eliminate all excuses for your bad attitudes. It's time to take responsibility for your choices. Life is a choice, and it begins with your attitude.
6. Hold firmly the remote control to your attitude. Others will try to take it from you and control your thoughts.
7. Find someone who can help you be accountable on a regular basis for your change in attitude.
8. Keep track of your progress. Record your daily goals and results in a journal.

Life is a choice, and it begins with your attitude.

Daily Attitude Check

To increase your awareness and understanding of your attitude, begin recording your thoughts and feelings on a daily basis over the next 30 days. The Attitude Action Planner on the following pages may be reproduced for your daily records.

> Just as you have a physical routine for getting ready each morning, take time to mentally prepare for the day.

Just as you have a physical routine for getting ready each morning, take time to mentally prepare for the day. Review your purpose and affirmation statements. Choose the kind of attitude you want for your day at home, at work, or at the ballpark. Identify ways in which you can adjust or maintain your attitude during the day.

At the end of each day, take time to end the day feeling good about yourself. Reflect and record your thoughts and feelings about the day. Give thanks for what went well. Identify what you learned and accomplished. To prepare your attitude for the next day, identify something you'll do again or do differently as a result of your day's experience.

Remember . . . attitude is your choice and you are just a choice away from gaining control of your attitude and your life.

Attitude Action Planner

Today is ______________________

Note:
Before you use this form, make several copies of it for your daily use.

At the beginning of each day . . .

- ☐ Start with a fresh attitude.
- ☐ Give thanks for another day to experience and enjoy.

✔ I feel ______________________ because I think ______________________

____

✔ My attitude for today:
I will be ______________________ because ______________________

____

✔ I will demonstrate my attitude today by: (Describe your specific actions.)

1. ______________________
2. ______________________
3. ______________________

✔ Through my attitude and actions today, I hope to enjoy these benefits and/or results:

1. ______________________
2. ______________________
3. ______________________

At the end of each day . . .

- ☐ Reward yourself.

✔ Today, I adjusted my attitude by: ______________________

____

____

✔ Today, I maintained my attitude by: ______________________

____

____

✔ Today, I dealt with someone else's difficult attitude by: ______________________

____

____

✔ Overall, I would evaluate my attitude today as: (*Check one*)

- ☐ Negative
- ☐ Neutral
- ☐ Positive

✔ From today's experience, I will maintain or adjust my attitude tomorrow by:

____

____

Other Learning Resources found at www.InspiringSolutions.com

The Attitude: The Choice is Yours[SM] *Advantage eLearning Course*

by Michele Matt

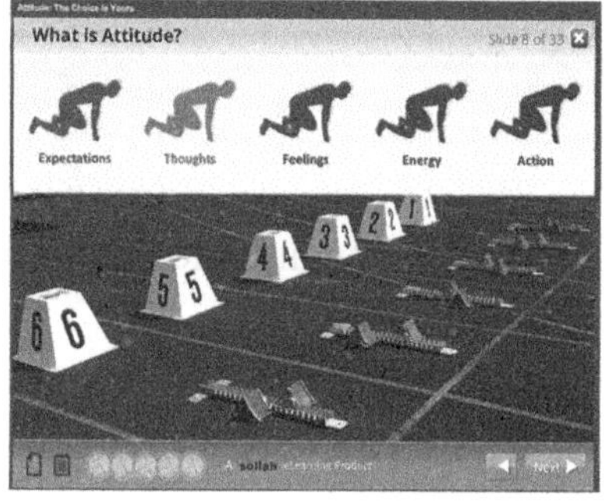

As a follow-up or companion resource with this book, enjoy an engaging and educational online course to gain control of your life by gaining control of your attitude. During the course, you will be running a "10K Race for the Attitude". Each mile completed helps you gain control over your attitude at work or at home by learning how to:

- Describe and recognize three types of attitudes.
- Use five attitude-adjustment techniques to improve the way you feel about yourself, change, other people, and responsibility.
- Implement five strategies for maintaining a positive attitude.
- Use a five-step process for dealing with a difficult attitude.

Attitude Control Bands®

A clever and fun way to remind yourself and other people how important it is to have a positive attitude. Thousands of people wear this rubber wrist band to "snap" themselves and others out of having a negative attitude. Give out at meetings or other learning experiences to stop "stinkin thinkin"!

Have your whole office or family wear them as an indication that we can control our life by controlling our attitude.

Other Learning Resources found at www.InspiringSolutions.com

Bad Apples™: How to Deal with Difficult Attitudes Kit

by Michele Matt

This award-winning video training program provides supervisors, managers and employees with practical techniques for confronting and eliminating negativity in the workplace. Kit includes a DVD with five vignettes, Facilitator Guide, Reproducible Participant Materials, and a Self-Study Guide which teaches how to:

- Recognize and describe the characteristics of a bad attitude.
- Understand how negativity impacts relationships and performance.
- Utilize a 5-step process for dealing with difficult people.

Activities to Enhance Good, Bad and Ugly Attitudes

by Michele Matt

Use this collection of 51 icebreakers and interactive projects to enhance good attitudes and improve bad and ugly attitudes. Reproducible handouts and exercises can be used with teams or individuals to:

- Enhance training.
- Stimulate a meeting.
- Inspire a coaching discussion.

Other Learning Resources found at www.InspiringSolutions.com

Personality Styles Mousepad

Use this as a quick desk reference guide to understand yourself and improve your relationship with others. Each of the DiSC® styles (Dominance, Influence, Steadiness and Conscientiousness) is described in terms of strengths, tendencies and needs/wants for working together. Use as a resource with these profiles:

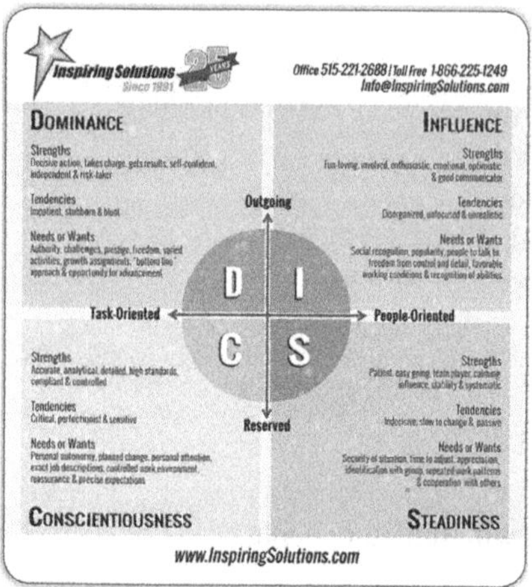

- DiSC Classic®
- Everything DiSC Workplace®
- Everything DiSC Management®
- Everything DiSC Sales®
- Everything DiSC Work of Leaders®
- Everything DiSC 363 for Leaders®

"DiSC," "Everything DiSC," "Everything DiSC Workplace," "Everything DiSC Work of Leaders," and "Everything DiSC 363 for Leaders" are trademarks of John Wiley & Sons, Inc.

Strategic Planning Handbook

by Michele Matt

This e-book is an excellent quick-read to explain a proactive approach to focus and recharge your leaders. Understand how to successfully develop and implement a strategic plan by utilizing a 10-step process to determine and define:

- Where are we now?
- Where are we going?
- How do we get there?
- How are we doing?